Speed Reading

Techniques and Hacks to Boost Your Reading Speed

(Increase Your Reading Speed by & Double Your Learning Skills in Less Than Hours)

James Wilson

Published By **Oliver Leish**

James Wilson

All Rights Reserved

Speed Reading: Techniques and Hacks to Boost Your Reading Speed (Increase Your Reading Speed by & Double Your Learning Skills in Less Than Hours)

ISBN 978-1-998901-23-4

No part of this guidebook shall be reproduced in any form without permission in writing from the publisher except in the case of brief quotations embodied in critical articles or reviews.

Legal & Disclaimer

The information contained in this ebook is not designed to replace or take the place of any form of medicine or professional medical advice. The information in this ebook has been provided for educational & entertainment purposes only.

The information contained in this book has been compiled from sources deemed reliable, and it is accurate to the best of the Author's knowledge; however, the Author cannot guarantee its accuracy and validity and cannot be held liable for any errors or omissions. Changes are periodically made to this book. You must consult your doctor or get professional medical advice before using any of the suggested remedies, techniques, or information in this book.

Table Of Contents

Chapter 1: What Is Speed Reading?

Most human beings typically have a tendency to equate pace reading with masterful skimming. However, it is inaccurate. In smooth phrases, velocity studying is a complicated technique of reading. Similar to the way in which the Olympics marathon is a complex form of cutting-edge potential – on foot, speed reading is a complex technique of studying. A runner in Olympics plays the same form of physical motion as any commonplace runner; but, it's far completed with extra average performance and quicker. The approach of velocity-analyzing abilties inside the equal manner. Now it's far clear that pace reading has no reference to skimming. Skimming involves skipping terms, which can't be regarded as a shape of pace reading.

What is Speed Reading?

As you've got a examine, it engages the ears, eyes, mind, and mouth. Speed studying engages all of those senses even more in assessment to everyday reading as you may be using your brainpower and senses in a more efficient manner. Speed analyzing is the technique of recognizing and soaking up sentences or phrases hastily on one net web page right away, in location of sincerely looking to come to be privy to separate phrases. The standard amount of statistics that someone can technique is developing every passing day, irrespective of if it's miles a file, e mail, website, book, magazine, or social media. Most mother and father will be inclined to experience compelled at the way to get via all such information speedy for staying within the loop. The majority of human beings can take a look at at an average charge of 250 words each minute; but, a few people would probably turn out to be quicker than others glaringly.

It is about seeing

The very first step this is available in reading some element is to look the words. However, do you genuinely see the phrases on an internet internet web page as you try to look at? In in advance researches, it come to be perception that human beings may additionally need to examine one word at one time. For studying, researchers idea that people commonly normally tend to move their eyes from left to proper at some point of one internet web page, know-how one phrase after each different. With this precept, speedy readers have been all those folks that can understand and discover phrases at a quicker charge. But beginner readers have the functionality to appearance greater and examine greater than a phrase at one time. As someone moves their eyes throughout an internet web page, they bounce in advance in suits and starts, accepting about one to 5 terms at one time in exquisite brief glances. Speed analyzing is primarily based on the following short glances:

• You have a look at diverse words in one glance until you undergo all such phrases that you aren't aware about or haven't encountered in advance than.
• You enlarge your imaginative and prescient so you can apprehend and test numerous phrases at one look.
• You make bigger your imaginative and prescient to take a look at texts vertically and furthermore horizontally on a page. Besides being capable of take in greater phrases, pace readers can also have a look at and understand phrases from or 3 lines at one glance.
It is set silent analyzing
As you study, you absolutely communicate words to your self as every body discover ways to observe with the technique of sound-it-out. When you have been in faculty, your teachers taught you that you may take a look at a phrase actually through sounding the

letters alongside side a mixture of letters. Having the capability to study out phrases is a crucial expertise for any type of novice reader. However, the nice hassle with this approach is that it is able to sluggish you down. You have a propensity to check not at the rate at which you suppose but on the charge at which you may communicate. Sounding out phrases is good sufficient for newbie readers; but, after a while, you can need to cast off sound in case you are willing to be a speed reader. Even saying the terms, that too whispering them on your head, takes a amazing deal of time. In pace analyzing, being attentive to and announcing terms as you hold reading is named vocalizing. Keep in thoughts that:

• Vocalizing has a connection in your early schooling of studying which you can need to abandon for being a speed reader.
• Training your self to not vocalize as you take a look at is one of the excessive

abilities of velocity studying that in reality all people can collect.

It is about comprehending

The most crucial cause of analyzing is to analyze and realize the whole thing which you observe. How well a person can recognize something they've a take a look at may be determined with the useful resource of the rate of analyzing, the degree of familiarity with the situation count number, and the vocabulary breadth. In a real experience, pace studying allows in improving your studying comprehension. As you have a look at out diverse terms at one time even as speed studying, you can pick out up the phrase meanings in the context. In reality, the method of velocity studying has a tendency to have some kind of snowball effect on the general length of preferred information and vocabulary, which complements your tempo of reading.

It is ready concentrating

Any form of analyzing desires cognizance. However, in velocity studying, the attention needs to be forceful and sustained as even as pace reading, you may need to do numerous subjects at one time. To well make use of the approach, you need to peer and look at all of the phrases on a web page, be alert to the writer's fundamental thoughts, anticipate with the writer, and encounter how he/she offers the written material. It is crucial to get a grip of the number one mind and observe out with greater angle for isolating out all styles of data from the heavier stuff. You will have to be aware about at the identical time as to take a look at rapid, on the identical time as to skim, and additionally at the equal time as to test slowly so that you can get an entire gist of the identical.

Challenges of Speed Reading
All human beings examine at numerous paces and in first-rate techniques. There are readers who can broaden the abilties

of studying in some weeks, whilst a few might likely take even longer to reach the extent of proficiency. But there are a few roadblocks to speed analyzing which you want to be privy to.

Insufficient vocabulary

The Third New International Dictionary from Webster includes about 470,000 phrases. Getting to understand they all is subsequent to not viable; but, growing your vocabulary will continuously beneficial resource your efforts of velocity reading. It is commonly encouraged to opt for the challenge of enhancing your vocabulary in a clever manner – search for one hundred – 120 immoderate-frequency terms that may be determined in books or other written materials that you discover hobby in. Also, you want to look out for phrases inside the dictionary as soon as you have carried out with a segment of the text, like a sentence or a paragraph. Keep in thoughts that you are most possibly to discover difficult terms in written language in assessment to speech. It is due to the truth writing is extra formal as regards to communication. Also, the human mind has a tendency to push aside all sorts of uncommon terms in spoken communique, filling the blanks with guesswork relying on the context.

One duration obtained't suit all

We all apprehend that the footwear of an athlete are custom designed counting on the foot of an character, hobby, and gait. In the equal way, the techniques of tempo analyzing are also required to be custom designed to the thoughts, the present degree of studying, the familiarity with the priority count number, and the text kind this is being tackled. Every form of reading fabric comes with its non-public patterns, rules, and worrying conditions. For instance, there are novels that have a look at the equal tale arc, at the same time as an unknown storyline may possibly without troubles slow you down as you determine on it to understand the equal.

Dense and nonfiction textbooks dive deep into subjects which is probably peculiar to the readers. They moreover need a pretty extraordinary tempo for absorbing the cutting-edge day piece of statistics. In truth, your platform of studying moreover subjects hundreds – e-books and articles might be a conflict for everybody with eye problems.

Every character's mind comes with a completely specific and awesome set of networks that arrived via genetic inheritance. It additionally develops due to the fact the end cease end result of learning and experience. In fact, the nearby language performs an important function within the development of your reading thoughts. Right in advance than you are making up your thoughts to have a examine a e-book, you need to reflect on the number one motive. What are the matters which you are trying to accumulate? Are you looking to examine to get to understand new information or for the verification of some detail? Are you seeking to read for leisure or schooling? Keep in thoughts that the purpose of analyzing will determine the approach set that you have to use.

The Basics

Learning new matters thru studying works wonderful for maximum humans. We all live in a quick-paced international in recent times. Information has a unethical to be the pivot of all forms of selections. So, it's miles quite essential to study the whole lot, proper from evaluations and files to emails, a wonderful deal faster than you sincerely do. Speed studying can be taken into consideration as a excessive manner to issues of this type. Gearing up the mind to take a look at faster is the number one critical step at the equal time as it comes to hurry analyzing.

Gearing up the Brain

You want to equipment up your thoughts on the way to observe texts at a quicker pace. There are certain strategies that you may study to conform the mind to faster behavior of reading. Let us have a have a look at such techniques.

The art work of skipping

Are you aware about the fact that the human mind is capable of expertise the essential idea of any form of subject matter with out even going through the lines? In case you study a few shape of nonfiction e-book, you could without problems get the overall form of the identical. You start with the advent and try to draw close the same with the aid of manner of manner of coronary coronary heart. Then, you opt for the subheads of the book. If you absolutely undergo the begin few strains or the closing line of the subheads, you could get to understand approximately 40 percent of the essential statistics that can be determined within the book. Such a strategy will assist you to have a look at quicker than ever.

Commanding the thoughts

You need to govern your thoughts as you check a topic. Try to be aware of the precept trouble really so the thoughts can capture it resultseasily. You need to connect to the appropriate phrases that might relate to a few form of sensible experience. For instance, in case you look at a few element concerning pressure manipulate, you might imagine of the pressure you have got skilled in lifestyles. In this manner, it'll be easier if you need to hyperlink with the state of affairs and store the same in your reminiscence.

Not subvocalizing as you examine

There are human beings who have the dependancy of mouthing some element they check. It has been observed that subvocalizing can without issues reduce your analyzing speed. If you moreover may have this type of addiction, you need to prevent it as speedy as possible. Try to have a look at the entirety mindfully, get to recognize the key terms, and you may bypass the rest.

Setting goals for capturing crucial facts

You want to invite yourself the purpose why you are studying a specific situation count number range. For instance, you're studying some thing that is based on workout. In this kind of case, you may need to be aware of your fitness dreams. You will must pick out out all the ones sections of the e-book that could help in conducting your goal. Your purpose have to be to observe all styles of facts on the way to gain you.

How Does the Brain Function as You Speed Read?

The 2d you come across effective terms on the time of studying some issue, the mind has a bent to hold the photograph and attempts to evaluate the whole thing. There are numerous research starting from the 365 days 1868 to the modern-day time that showed reading as a completely intellectual technique. Also, it has no hyperlink with subvocalization. So, in case you want to beautify your analyzing pace, you'll ought to attempt to exercising with none shape of subvocalization. It is usually recommended to make a addiction of reading just a few terms at one time in region of seeking to take a look at every phrase. It will in reality assist in increasing your tempo of analyzing.

Normal Reading and Brain

As you look at some issue, to peer the terms, you operate your eyes, to test and articulate the phrases, you use your pharynges and tongue, to pay interest what you take a look at, you use your ears, and to assess the semantics of the terms you operate your thoughts. You might not have a look at aloud; but, you pronounce and observe the terms in your mind. So, subvocalization may be appeared as part of our dependancy of studying that develops from formative years. As you observe a few element, generally, your mind capabilities on the ones:

• Processing of visual information: When we observe, that statistics that we see with our eyes is inside the layout of phrases. Our mind takes the photo and additionally starts offevolved strolling on the identical. The mind techniques each phrase, determines them and moreover stores them in the reminiscence issue.
• Processing of acoustic records: The phrases that someone reads get recorded inside the reminiscence of the mind in the form of acoustic records in a few particular language. In clean phrases, as you take a look at or pay attention a few element acoustically, the mind starts offevolved offevolved encoding the visual imagery of the phrases inside the shape of acoustic facts.
• Processing of semantic information: Our mind analyzes the acoustic along thing the seen facts with the help of language that is seemed to us. It

moreover determines the relational because of this that can be discovered among the acoustic and visible message. After that, we are able to understand the real that means of what we study.

The thoughts desires a while to approach those three steps. Thus, it develops a barrier in the method of ordinary reading.

Processing Visual Information

As you word some thing at the time of reading, the mind captures all of the seen records of the terms. After, the statistics gets processed. So, it is able to be stated that the processing of visible facts is the capability of the mind to research and technique the entirety which you see. After the thoughts is completed with analyzing the statistics, the equal receives saved inside the reminiscence so that you can go through in mind it on any future occasion. The pace at which you look at any shape of statistics is certainly depending on the capability of your thoughts to method statistics. The quantity of your mind's functionality to be sturdy is all that allows in figuring out how as it have to be and quick you get to have interaction with the environment and situations you're uncovered to. So, processing of visible records is all about:

• The thoughts's notion, cognition, and wonderful activities let you revel in, decide the that means, and understand everything which you see.
• Processing of facts that includes automatic reputation of everything your eyes test. In general, human eyes stay on any phrase or object for about one-fourth of a 2d and then moves without delay to the subsequent word or object. In case the thoughts can not discover the phrase or the item name that you see at the side of your eyes, your eyes get decrease again to the phrase or item over again and reread the identical for popularity. The eyes will keep getting

decrease lower back to the equal detail until the mind can understand it.

• Inability to decide and take a look at the statistics may additionally stand up if you have were given some problems, consisting of binocular instability or eye-tracking contamination. In such times, you may need clinical guidance and remedy.

Factors Limiting the Brain's Capacity to Speed Read

There are positive elements that could restriction the capacity of the mind to look at with pace. Such elements may also growth the time of processing seen facts inside the mind. Some of them are referred to below.

• Fixation: As we've a have a look at, the eyes deliver interest to terms and additionally stay on them for approximately 3 milliseconds. During this time, if one line includes ten terms and the phrases embody 5 letters on common, the eyes will take approximately 4 seconds to have a look at that line.

• Saccade: The 2d you take a look at some element, it might be the case that your frame is at relaxation, the top is steady to recognition on terms that you read. However, the eyes will now not be at relaxation. If you ever try to revel in what the eyes do, you may find out that they glance at the phrases. Such a jerky movement of the eyes is known as a saccade. Each saccade includes visible tiers that may accommodate 8 letters at one time in massive. The human eyes take approximately zero.Three seconds for every saccade movement.

• Acoustical processing: The studying tempo that you have has an inclination to get low due to the acoustical processing of the thoughts. It consists of acquiring terms, records encoding, garage of statistics within the reminiscence, and records extraction with the assist of reencoding. All of those are the essential elements of the acoustic functioning of the thoughts as you try and have a examine a few text. So, mouthing and articulation of terms reduce the speed of the eyes at which they look the phrases.

- Subvocalization: We use the vocal cords as we look at. There are humans who've the dependancy of analyzing aloud. As you look at, you now not pleasant pronounce all the words in your mind; however, you moreover mght pay hobby the identical to your ear. The need for listening to the terms which you observe and observe, which are not that critical on the time of reading, slows down your studying tempo.

Overcoming the Limiting Barriers

Today, we live in a quick-paced worldwide wherein it's miles crucial to test a outstanding deal of data than in advance than for getting completed with all styles of artwork. So, it may be said that it's far the need of the time for us to have a look at at faster speeds. In famous, we're capable of have a look at approximately one hundred fifty to two hundred phrases every minute, wherein you may have the need to look at approximately seven hundred − 800 terms each minute. Is there any possible way of wearing out this? Here are some of the techniques in which you may triumph over the bounds to rush studying.

Using a finger to guide the eyes as you've got a take a look at

To get started out out out with a very new approach of analyzing, you could start studying at the same time as using your finger to guide the eyes as you examine. As you do so, it will help the thoughts to take in a set of phrases in region of studying each word. In fact, it is able to moreover assist in minimizing subvocalization.

Distracting the tongue and mouth for pronunciation

You want to distract your thoughts from the pronunciation of the words and saying the identical to the thoughts. In order to save you such an vintage addiction, you could keep chewing a few gum in your mouth as you examine, for example. It will help in minimizing subvocalization to a exceptional diploma. Listening to music as you observe

It acts as a super shape of remedy at the time of reading. Such a exercise can also help in developing your reputation as you take a look at whilst lowering subvocalization at the same time. It is suggested to select some form of classical track for the cut price of subvocalization.

Using RSVP packages

There is a few useful software software software program software for tempo analyzing that could provide you with all of the help you want to beautify your analyzing pace thru decreasing subvocalization. All such programs are smooth to apply and smooth. They use

Rapid Serial Visual Presentation to decorate your pace of reading.

Speed of Reading

Have you bought pretty a few paperwork to test inside a remaining date that keeps stalking you all the time? Do you have got masses of analyzing to do? Is it vital if you want to simply look at faster, whether or now not it's far for paintings or private requirements? But how is it feasible to have a look at faster? Here are some validated techniques so one can allow you to enhance your pace of reading pretty resultseasily and without lots trouble.

Stopping the Internal Monologue
Your internal monologue, termed subvocalization, is a totally commonplace trait that can be observed among readers. It consists of talking every phrase on your thoughts as you examine

some detail. In truth, it's far frequently considered the maximum crucial impediment that could come among you and enhancing your studying velocity. In case you pay hobby voices to your mind as you study, there may be no longer something to freak out. As prolonged as it's miles your voice, reading with you, there is not a few element to worry approximately. It is the manner wherein teachers ask kids to look at — pronouncing the phrases silently in thoughts as they test. As we get taught to observe some thing to begin with, we're taught to sound out every possible thing and take a look at the equal loudly. It is the manner in which the dependancy of subvocalization originates, and the majority oldsters preserve reading in this manner.

But you need to triumph over this in case you are willing to decorate your speed. The common pace of studying is greater or a good deal much less similar to the commonplace speed of talking. It has been positioned that the commonplace tempo of analyzing for adults is ready three hundred terms each minute. As most human beings have the addiction of announcing all the phrases loudly of their mind on the time of analyzing, they check on the equal pace as they communicate. It suggests that you can growth your tempo of analyzing to the quantity you hold up the inner monologue. In case you really need to enhance your tempo, you could have to cast off your internal monologue.

Chunking Words
It is greater or less like doing away with the inner monologue. It involves the act of studying numerous phrases at one time, and it's far one of the keys to study faster. In fact, it is one of the nice device that may be used for boosting your tempo of analyzing. An individual can soak up more than one terms at once. Utilizing your peripheral vision is one of

the strategies wherein you can make this step even less difficult. We will talk about that later. For this, try and pay attention to studying three phrases with a look. Keep doing this till you attain the stop of the web web page, and take a be aware about how speedy you can entire an internet web web page. You will even though be able to understand and method everything you take a look at; however, you will be spending tons much less time doing this.

Now, you want to take the technique one step in advance. Take one pencil and draw parallel strains vertically down the web page of textual content, separating the web web page text into 3 precise sections. Start from the pinnacle left as you generally do, and use paper or your hand to cover the whole thing underneath the line. Concentrate on studying the text of every segment as a unmarried hassle. Your cause is to chunk the phrases collectively and take a look at them at one look, similar to you do with a road sign. Continue doing this as you bypass down the page. You will quickly recognize that your studying pace turned into faster in evaluation to earlier than. You can maintain doing this until you get cushty sufficient to task your self with a few component more.

Utilizing Peripheral Vision
You will now research the important component method that lets in in tying the whole thing in a unmarried location. Indeed, it isn't the very last step, however it's miles a crucial one. You need to start thru way of the use of the techniques above to look and apprehend diverse phrases straight away. In region of chunking smaller word corporations, you may ought to attempt to look at one line right now. It includes searching proper on the center of a line and placing into use the peripheral vision so that you can results take a look at the closing of it. You will need to test the whole internet

web page on this form of manner, and as you get to the lowest of the internet web page, you may see that you can no matter the truth that apprehend everything which you take a look at, that too in file time!

No Rereading of Words on a Page
In case you may have a check the eyes of someone as they observe, you'll see that they jump and flit. You will even note that they do not go with the go with the flow in an splendid manner, back and forth, within the way they have to. It is due to the reality a median character has the tendency to enter reverse phrases that they have got already look at. It is one of the matters that might without issue prevent you from increasing your tempo of studying. Most folks generally will be inclined to try this with out even being capable of realise the same, which makes it a hard addiction to close down. Well, the very satisfactory way of dealing with it's far to use a finger or any

bookmark to guide you. It can also sound infantile, but it truly works like marvel. You want to keep taking walks your finger to and fro all through an internet page with out in search of to save you or going once more. You will want to keep song of the phrases due to the fact the finger keeps making its way down the internet page textual content content. As you reap the save you, try and preserve in thoughts what you look at. You did no longer even try and get lower once more over any single phrase, and although, you may preserve in thoughts everything.

Opting for a Timer

When it comes to "file time," now could be the chance to test out your self and additionally art work on the processes wherein you could decorate your pace of studying every time. You can do that with the useful resource of setting a timer for a minute, reading as you do as time passes via. The 2nd the timer goes off, try and find out the variety of pages you have finished. You need to keep doing this and try to beat your past depend every time. You can also set a weekly or each day goal, except treating yourself on every occasion you achieve the reason. With the assist of this clean activity, you may growth your tempo of studying proper away the least bit.

Reading More

We are all privy to the pronouncing, "Practice have to make some thing excellent." It is quite correct for each problem of life. Any artist, professional, musician, or special individuals exercise all of the time which will enhance themselves. As a reader, you want to do the equal. Keep in mind that the greater you may look at, the better you'll be at it. At the same time, the better you could be at studying, the more you could decorate your tempo.

Using Marker

Do you observed that your imaginative and prescient keeps slipping and sliding through a web web page as you attempt to observe? If that is the case, there can be not something to worry about. Just area one index card below each line, and maintain slipping it down as you keep reading. It will make sure which you do no longer get defocused even as studying a line and now not taking some thing in.

Skimming the Key Points First
When you've got got were given a brief amount of time, and you require to have a look at a few aspect internal a deadline, take deep breaths and try to calm yourself down. Open the web web page of text which you want to observe and take it slow to look at all of the number one elements. Now, examine the contents, subtitles, captions which can be available under the diagrams, or some different form of text. The intention have to be to get a entire experience of the segment or

bankruptcy, or textual content. Now, have a look at the number one paragraph of every number one section. You will need to test the center and the last. Try to assume this over on your mind and region them collectively as a unmarried piece. Next, start studying the entirety the use of the strategies that we have already referred to above. In this way, you will get to preserve any form of data in a higher way, besides developing your speed of studying.

Chapter 2: Conceptualization And Visualization

Visualization is the crucial energy to increase highbrow imagery and to enhance your normal overall performance along side gaining knowledge of. Visual imagery is not unusual for memory, creativeness, and daydreaming. However, there are folks who discover it difficult to soak up such seen snap shots. Due to this, they generally will be inclined to face troubles in performing or studying any form of hobby. Not being able to draw up highbrow pix is termed "congenital aphantasia." Keep in mind that intellectual imagery plays an crucial function in analyzing new meanings and for analyzing comprehension. Mental imagery can offer you with all of the assist to absorb requirements of all kinds of summary things. With the use of mind maps, you may keep and maintain in thoughts critical data.

How to Opt for Effective Visualization?
Visualization allows in enhancing the abilties of studying comprehension so that you can collect more information via text know-how. We can visualize text automatically as we hold education using this kind of capacity. As you visualize at the same time as reading, you may get the risk to accumulate an remarkable studying experience and hold in thoughts the entirety you examine. When an individual hears or reads a few sort of textual content by way of way of the use of visualization, they could hyperlink themselves to the real text. For example, all the ones who've a have a look at storybooks can get engaged with the characters of the tale as they are capable of in fact recall the characters. Such a thing can help them to get the revel in of right reading besides getting all of the encouragement to hold reading the

book. It is quite smooth to get started with working in the direction of visualization. All you need to do is to choose out a text that consists of descriptive languages and strong verbs.

You can begin from a detail an excellent manner to offer you all help to conjure targeted pix. Well, there may be no requirement to get worried in a whole book at the begin. You have were given the selection to choose a few well installed sentenced or any paragraph so that you can begin with the lesson of visualization. There are certain strategies that can be decided.

How Are Meanings Created?
The syntax of the English language isn't always that tough. In order to amplify sentences complete of which means that, you can require primary components – an actor/ assignment and an motion. The closer the 2 additives are located in a sentence, the simpler it's

going to possibly be as a manner to identify them. Try to decide the verb, and the mission on this sentence – Prince Joseph made a promise to Prince Adam to go back to his birthday party. Here, Prince Joseph is the concern or actor of the sentence. The actor is doing some motion, that is promising. The promise is the verb within the sentence. It is crucial that that verb and the problem are associated with every special grammatically in a sentence to make experience. But what's Prince Adam in the sentence? Well, it is the item this is receiving the movement, and "to come lower back to his birthday party" is a collection of greater phrases.

Start Reading

The exceptional way of combatting barriers associated with lengthy sentences is to lower the sentence. While we have were given in no manner been free from distractions, from dealing with the ringing telephones and lumps of mails to dealing with own family problems, the distractions have never been so overwhelming, voluminous, continual, and extreme as they will be now. Ringing cellular phones are one difficulty; but, social media messages, electronic mail notifications, severa digital devices, and numerous browser tabs open are quite some different. The extra we're related, the extra we're up for the neck of statistics, and the greater we take part in the battle of interest. We will be inclined to get engaged in the blur of multitasking sports activities.

As we artwork, we're coping with distractions that come from every possible route. So, in case you need to hurry have a look at and apprehend the text's right that means, you can should unfastened yourself from the distractions. As you test, try to discover the kind of sentences inside the text, the length of the sentences, the presence of punctuations, and then relate to the overall which means that. It will help your mind look at the text and paint an extensive photograph of the overall content material material. Try to turn out to be aware about the number one components of a sentence, like a verb, situation, item, or supplement, and extra clusters will assist to unpack the which means faster. All of those will will will can help you navigate the hard substances without issues.

Myths of Speed Reading

If you have ever heard of a person speakme approximately the manner in which they completed fifty books in three hundred and sixty 5 days, it'd sound not possible. Or, a colleague of yours completing a fifty-net web page document in a single hour on the identical time as you need double the time to finish the identical element. As you evaluate your self with them, you may try and parent out the methods wherein they attain this. It may also furthermore be the case that their agenda is packed much like yours. Well, how packed is the calendar of a person has no relation to how fast they may take a look at. For example, CEO and investor of Berkshire and Hathaway, Warren Buffet, can have a look at approximately six hundred – a thousand pages each day. How can a person spend plenty time reading? People who can in reality fly thru any shape of textual content can achieve this with the assist of speed-reading techniques. You want to have heard numerous subjects approximately the concept of pace studying. But maximum of them are myths. We will speak a number of the commonplace myths of pace analyzing in this economic catastrophe.

Reading More Than 500 Words Every Minute Is Not Possible

The average reading tempo of an person is ready 2 hundred – 250 terms each minute. In reality, there are adults who can have a look at extra than 500 phrases every minute. Also, the quantity of studying that any excessive-degree government does is over 575 phrases in keeping with minute. Professors spend a superb deal of time studying, wherein they may be capable of look at approximately 675 phrases each minute. Of route, there are people who train themselves for competitions of tempo analyzing. For example, Anne Jones, the champion of the sector tempo-studying opposition, can examine approximately 4700 phrases each minute besides comprehending about sixty eight% of the overall text. As you begin, you may no longer be at the volume of Anne Jones. There is not anything to melancholy as you can with out problem decorate your studying tempo with exercising and time.

You Can Comprehend More While Reading Slowly

In evaluation to the well-known perception, analyzing at a gradual velocity will now not assist you with comprehension. In truth, gradual reading can harm the amount of text that you may recognize. Comprehension has little or now not some thing to do with the charge at which a person reads. It has extra to do with whether or not you could decipher and additionally maintain the data which you study. One of the primary skills that every velocity reader learns is to preview the to be had textual content in advance than reading and amplify a mind map.

You Can Enjoy More As You Read Slowly

It is a very commonplace misconception that it's miles really fake and has no basis the least bit. As you study slowly, your mind can get distracted greater with out issues. It may additionally bring about boredom, in which you may emerge as freeing your thoughts to wander spherical. Try to consider it in this way – you'll in no manner download some film and try to watch it in sluggish movement. The same element applies to reading. As you preserve a brief pace whilst studying a piece file or novel, it could make the examine extra energizing. Speed reading is all about green studying. As you observe fast, you will be a higher reader. Also, you could get extra pleasure alongside factor meaning out of the articles, books, and blogs which you take a look at. In fact, there are those who increase great love for reading best as they discover ways to pace study.

You Will Have to Skip Words to Read Faster

As you pace take a look at, you may ought to organisation terms collectively in region of skipping them. It may additionally appear that word grouping isn't always any better than word skipping; however, it can do the trick.

How you could gain this is a few other wonderful method of speed studying that you have already decided out in the preceding chapters.

Speed Reading Is Supernatural
Any character can research the strategies wherein they may be capable of pace examine. Try to count on what it would feel like if you may get thru any shape of textbook as you examine the strategies of reading about 1500 words or more each minute, similar to any commonplace tempo reader. Speed reading also can enhance your comprehension, decorate your abilities of productivity, and improve your reminiscence. All of those are enough reasons to attempt out the technique of tempo analyzing.

Slow Reading Can Enhance Your Concentration
People of nowadays's technology come across the majority of records inside the

shape of visuals and texts very slowly as they regard it because the manner to research, understand, and apprehend. However, on the same time, at the equal time as an individual is given a unique to finish, he/she reads the identical at a quicker price and might although apprehend the number one concept of the story. You need to recollect that there are various phrases in paragraphs and sentences that aren't that important all of the time. They are alleged to be have a look at for the thoughts and now not for the terms. So, there can be no relation amongst analyzing slowly and interest.

Everyone Read at Their Natural Speed
Some humans bear in mind that reading is a talents that we all are born with. So, it's far frequently said that sluggish reading or velocity analyzing consists of us clearly. However, to keep in mind this scientifically, it is been confirmed that analyzing generates from mastering. The

skills of studying may also range from one character to the alternative. For example, at the same time as people power a car, they strength at unique speeds. The reason within the once more of that is that they have got discovered out to power in any other case, and it isn't a few aspect that involves them manifestly. So, it could be stated that there may be nothing referred to as "herbal pace studying."

You Always Need a Pacer to Speed Read
A pacer can be regarded as a seen manual, like a pen or finger, that allows mark in that you study on an internet page. There are human beings who have a stereotypical picture of someone pace studying as a loopy-looking person who maintains dragging their finger or a pacer down the web page for the act of studying. But you received't want a pacer for pace studying. Using a pacer can satisfactory be useful sooner or later of the early tiers of pace studying. You

abandon the same as you get a right maintain of the approach.

Now which you are nicely aware of the common myths and misconceptions associated with velocity studying, try and supply it a circulate for your self. All you want is staying power and staying power. You received't be a grasp of speed studying internal a few hours or days. But you may have a have a look at the strategies interior a few months.

Chapter 3: Reduction Of Subvocalization

Subvocalization is quite not unusual among all readers. It is all approximately announcing phrases inside the mind as you examine, and additionally it is one of the essential motives why maximum human beings have gradual studying speed. It moreover makes it tough to decorate one's analyzing pace. There are masses of tempo-reading programs that will be inclined to exaggerate and falsely declare that the primary key to developing your studying pace is to discard subvocalization. But it's far been placed from various research that removal of this form of addiction in reality isn't always viable. We will speak the manner in which readers can lessen subvocalization in this segment. As you limit your subvocalization inclinations, you may with out hassle boost up your tempo of studying. In fact, it can help in improving your comprehension.

Do You Hear Voices in Your Mind While Reading?

When we were taught to take a look at all through our teenagers days, we have been cautioned to check the whole thing aloud. As to procure fluent enough, your teacher might possibly have instructed you to say the terms which you examine to your mind. It is the way in which the overall dependancy of subvocalization has an inclination to originate in popular. The majority of humans keep studying in this way for his or her entire lives. However, in case you are willing to increase your studying pace, you will should lessen this sort of dependancy. There isn't always any need to mention each phrase which you examine for your mind to understand the which means. When you were young, it modified into important to duplicate every single word in your head. However, with growing age, you may now determine the because of this that of the terms sincerely thru looking at them. You are no longer required to pronounce the phrases aloud on your thoughts so that you can get the equal sort of know-how.

But there might be situations at the identical time as you will be predisposed to take a look at without announcing the phrases to your thoughts. For example, reflect onconsideration on the instances whilst you strain. As you see a red signal, do you have a tendency to subvocalize the phrase "forestall" on your mind? You ought to have completed so within the second ass you test the word in the sentence; however, as you come upon a prevent signal on the time of driving, your opportunities of pronouncing the phrase are nil. You have a look on the sign and recognize it mechanically that it is a sign to forestall. In case you are like the bulk of readers, you would possibly subvocalize maximum or all the terms within the thoughts. However, you couldn't subvocalize all of the time everything which you look at. Let us have a have a look at one greater instance.

Suppose you're reading a few difficulty and stumble upon the yea "1987," you will no longer say for your mind "Nineteen Eighty-Seven." You are maximum possibly to understand the one year simply via manner of having a have a look at the range. Or, in case you stumble upon the range "3, 546, 789," you may now not subvocalize the identical into terms. For the type of huge variety, you have got got a look at it, and you can apprehend that it is a huge one. Such an records comes quite brief. There isn't any need to subvocalize the range. But in case you do, you'll be looking the enormous range for quite some time without making any kind of development inside the sentence.

It Is All About Ideas

Reading has not a few component to do with terms. However, it's far all about the extraction of thoughts, getting statistics, and soaking up important information. Words themselves won't mean some aspect except they arrive surrounded via way of a few considered one of a kind terms. As you have a look at "New York City," do you located of it as 3 separate terms? The majority parents might probable without a doubt equate the phrases to a city. In fact, NYC should advise the equal element. Right? We see severa phrases which may be simplest used for grammar, together with a, an, the. They ought to no longer offer you with the same kind of which means due to the fact the phrase "college." You want to reduce subvocalization to reinforce up your studying pace. But what is the cause at the back of this? It is due to the fact subvocalization can effortlessly limit how fast someone may have a examine.

You can think of it on this way – in case you say each word on your thoughts, does now not that indicate that you can only observe at the price at which you could speak? In case you have a propensity to say every phrase to your mind, your restrict might be the charge at which you talk.

Reading Speed Is Equals to Talking Speed

The common velocity of reading for most parents is about one hundred sixty – 250 phrases each minute. The average pace of speaking is extra or a exquisite deal a whole lot much less the same. As maximum human beings say terms of their minds as they examine, they commonly will be inclined to examine at a similar charge in which they talk. It is possible to test it out on our very private. Try to have a look at typically for one minute, after which attempt to check out loud for a minute. In case you are like maximum human beings, your speakme pace and analyzing pace may be the identical. If the fee at that you have a look at exceeds the rate of speaking, that is a top notch thing. No one desires to get restrained to his/her speakme pace. What is the cause inside the lower again of maximum human beings analyzing round 100 fifty – 250 terms steady with minute and no longer something above 3 hundred? It is because it is hard to talk that speedy.

Unless you are habituated to disclaimers that may be placed at the forestall of commercials, it is not in any respect easy to talk extra than 3 hundred phrases each minute. So, you want to lessen subvocalization to keep away from getting stuck with studying as speedy as you speak. In truth, you've got had been given were given the electricity to read as rapid as you suspect. Altering the addiction of subvocalization is a whole lot less hard said than being completed.

You can't turn down the voice on your thoughts. In area of looking to remove the addiction, you can preference to reduce the identical.

How Can Subvocalization Be Useful at Times?

Repeating and announcing terms to your thoughts may be useful at instances. For example, as you have a look at a few material that includes technical vocabulary or terminology that you are not used to. In such conditions, as you repeat terms in your thoughts or perhaps say them aloud, it can be a extraordinary way to enhance and make bigger your vocabulary. There is some different way in which subvocalization may be beneficial. In case you want to memorize some trouble word through phrase, searching for to subvocalize the associated words or announcing the terms aloud can assist. How do you found that the actors do not forget the lengthy dialogues? It is all finished with the assist of subvocalization. Reading out loud can help in memorizing a few component phrase thru phrase.

However, at the identical time as you look at normally, you could hardly ever need to understand some element by using method of each word. The majority of the time, you test is to extract ideas, data, and critical records. In order to beautify up your pace of studying, you may need to lessen subvocalization with the aid of using trying to say just a few words in every line. In case you attempt to say each word, you can get limited to the speakme speed. But how are you going to recognize that the dependancy is converting? If you begin with analyzing 3oo phrases each minute, you may be clear which you are saying every word to your mind, and this is why the word do not forget is low. However, if the remember range goes as a good deal as 4 hundred terms regular with minute, you could regard it as unique improvement.

Ways of Minimizing Subvocalization

Here are sure tips that you could look at.

Using your hand to guide the eyes on the time of analyzing

You ought to have heard experts stressing to apply your hand so that you can guide your eyes. Well, it is able to be appeared as a number one precept of all types of tempo-reading strategies and can be very powerful that could help lessen subvocalization. As you use your hand to guide your imaginative and prescient, it may assist in grabbing a number of phrases on the time of analyzing, at the identical time as supporting you to deal with every other dependancy of reading – fixation.

Distracting your self

In order to reduce subvocalization, you may try to distract your self from pronouncing all of the phrases to your thoughts. But how can someone distract themself? There are nice strategies of doing this. One of the best methods is to have chewing gum as you take a look at. It will save you you from repeating terms for your head. Also, subvocalization isn't simplest approximately the internal voice. Your tongue, ears, larynx, and lips all play a few position in the desired approach. But if you could distract all such organs, you'll be capable of reduce subvocalization. You can distract your ears on the identical time as reading with slight song. Stay far from loud track. You can preserve your larynx occupied by way of using smooth buzzing with the music.

Scanning earlier than reading

To reduce subvocalization, it is probably useful to understand complicated phrases or surprising terminologies. The number one concept is to test the available textual content quickly earlier than you make a decision to get into detail. One of the methods of doing this is to perform a fantastic quick check the usage of your fingers and draw an "S" form throughout and down the complete web page. You will need to strain the eyes to track the pinnacle of your finger. The fundamental purpose of one of these test isn't to gain notion; but, to select out up all types of regular phrases and phrases. As you come across one, subvocalize it intentionally. As you start studying, your possibilities of subvocalization might be a whole lot much less.

Occupying the internal voice with a few other element

As it is not possible to take away subvocalization absolutely, the terrific problem that can be carried out on your issue is to hold your inner voice busy with unique duties. One of the handiest approaches of doing so is to recollect to your mind as you start studying. As you maintain counting 1, 2, three... to your thoughts on the identical time as studying, your inner voice will now not get sufficient time to be privy to the textual content that you are trying to procedure. It also can seem a chunk difficult in the beginning; however, after a while, you'll understand that you could observe quicker with out even finding the repetitive list distracting.

The Technique of Reduced Margin

The majority of found out material that we come across has margins – the gap that lies some of the actual text at the internet web page and the threshold of the net page. When online articles first got here into being, the programmers of the web sites underestimated the want of margins on the a part of readers. They ended up populating the internet internet page with pages that protected no margins the least bit. After some years, it come to be clean that margins can very well impact the readability of any form of virtual textual content. Margins were then added to all types of internet websites and templates. Indeed, margin-much much less pages at the internet can although be decided, however it is clear in recent times that which incorporates massive white place round any shape of textual content is crucial for clarity.

Reduced Margin

As we already stated that margins are crucial, then why is it had to lessen the same? Although having margins is crucial for clean analyzing, you need to realize that they do not have any textual content and so there can be no want for sharp foveal vision. Peripheral vision can do all of the duties as all which you need from margins is to decide in which traces begin and quit. In order to take whole benefit of your peripheral vision on text margins, you could start to circulate in or indent the preliminary and very last fixations on each line. You want to do this deliberately. For making it look tons less hard, try to bear in mind vertical strains that run down the web web page right over the text, half of of an inch from the outward region.

Here is the manner in which the attention motion of a reader alters as they use the method of reduced margin. Below are lines with and with out the approach of reduced margin. If each of the highlighted areas denotes a fixation, is it possible which will wager which one is which?

The climate stepped forward after the drought, and the weather have become searching promising for the plants.

The climate progressed after the drought, and the climate changed into looking promising for the vegetation.

Try to phrase that the number one example has handiest four fixations, while the second one has six. Naturally, you can take a look at the number one sentence quicker. With this, you may understand that the primary instance used the method of decreased margin and the second instance did no longer.

The Parafovea

The method of decreased margin wishes the activation of a ultra-modern eye location, the parafovea. It is like a skinny belt that can be found across the fovea, the retina aspect that is usually used for analyzing. Well, it isn't that sensitive to facts similar to the fovea. Also, it cannot distinguish terms. But the parafovea comes with the capability to find out shapes and is advanced to the opportunity eye factors. The retina is composed of each other outdoor belt referred to as the perifovea. It also performs the a part of peripheral imaginative and prescient. Parafoveal vision is a peripheral vision that uses the vicinity of parafovea vicinity – decided many of the fovea and perifovea. It is worried inside the characteristic of figuring out fixations.

As it comes with the capacity to discover shapes, the parafovea can very effortlessly examine the phrase shapes and clusters. It makes predictions concerning a higher landing for the upcoming eye fixation. As you optimize your fixations, you'll be capable of reduce the giant shape of stops on each line. Thus, you could moreover maximize your comprehension. Keep in mind that the improvement of parafoveal vision calls for time alongside aspect plenty of schooling. It is just like any new dependancy. So, you may practice the use of your cloth for multiple months so that you can acquire considerable improvement. As you begin, you could draw vertical strains using a pencil so you can remind your mind to reduce the margins.

Advanced Parafoveal Reading

You can utilize the retinal outer edge place now not best to lessen the variety of fixations on each line; but, moreover to preview the available material in advance. As you study a few text, your eyes view the regions and terms which can be present at the contemporary-day line. The thoughts and retina seize two or 3 strains which may be outside the location of foveal imaginative and prescient. You can efficiently faucet into this facts so that you provide yourself with the needed help to preview the text lying ahead. You also can plan the fixation stops. As already stated in advance, perifoveal and parafoveal imaginative and prescient aren't that sharp similar to the foveal. However, they could but signal within the bounds and shapes of the terms quite well. Certain terms, together with "every now and then" and "statistics," consist of a particular shape on the side of duration. Prepositions, inclusive of "at," "in," and "of," are quick in length that is surrounded by means of the usage of white regions. They can also symbolize the starting of a cluster. With continuous practice, the brain can be made higher to sign in them with the help of peripheral

vision and furthermore alter the actions
of the eyes as a result.

Chapter 4: Layered Reading

The famous approach of layered reading consists of 3 steps – test out, take a look at, and mirror. We will speak the techniques wherein you could enhance your normal general performance in terms of harder texts with the usage of the layered reading technique.

Reading is often seemed as an act of empathy. No do not forget in case you look at a fictional e-book or a nonfictional one, the writer will take you on a journey. Your simplest task inside the position of a reader is to look at alongside. You will enjoy some of the trips which can be like taking walks inside the park, at the same time as others might be like a tough run that consists of an obstacle path. Walking within the park received't require any sort of unique plan, however hard races may want to require a map that you may believe. Such a map is needed to be determined in advance with the usage of GPS. When writers do now not provide the readers with any form of a clean map or a GPS device to apprehend their writing, they regularly depart again severa clues which will let you gather your map and high the thoughts to study. So, in case you want to understand a writer's argument in any e-book, you may need to first choose the book as an inspector.

Inspect

To get started out out, have a look at the perceive of the book collectively with the subtitle. You will need to don't forget what the e-book is all about in advance than you even decide to open it. What do you experience the author is trying to deliver concerning the problem on the quilt? After that, have a have a observe the date of book. It is essential if you pick out a few form of time-touchy fabric, along side technical publications or clinical research. You might even regulate your mind concerning analyzing the e-book if it modified into published an prolonged in the past and won't be relevant to the cutting-edge-day time. You may additionally want to maintain a word concerning the publisher of the e-book. When you come across self-posted titles, it's miles crucial to bear in mind that each one those books which have a author undergo rigorous checking and improving.

It is critical to usually try to have a observe with a important eye. However, it's miles particularly important as you check a few self-posted books. On the alternative, books which can be posted through huge publishers are most likely to be unique. As who the writer is, you will be capable of vicinity the e-book in a few elegance mentally. Keep in mind that the extra you have a look at, the more you can get a few enjoy for it. Indeed, it's far the writer or the author who offers a book with a special identity. So, it's miles important to have a observe the background. What are the topics that make the author an expert on the trouble? Why ought to a person pay attention to the message of the author? You also can choose some internet research. While a few interviews of the author could probably have very little or no longer whatever to do with the text which you need to take a look at, it could be a terrific way of getting a gist of the author's argument.

As authors have the tendency of the use of the extraordinary examples from all their books inside the interviews, they could act as the extraordinary primer for the thoughts. As you begin to take a look at something with some pre-acquired data regarding the attitude of the writer, it can assist in comprehending the content material cloth material of the book greater all at once.

Treat the table of contents like a map

Do you consider what we stated within the preceding section concerning the author supplying a map for their argument? Where is the book seeking to take you to? What are the strategies in which are getting there? How many small components or huge additives are present in the argument? Well, everything may be determined in the table of contents. It is pretty first-rate to look that most humans normally have a tendency to dive into direct analyzing without even having a have a examine the internet web web page of contents. The writers spend a first rate quantity of time bobbing up with a right outline. In reality, nonfiction books can not be presented without a unique desk of contents. Even the define is generally constant; it's far a better concept to discover which quantities make up the easy percent of the writing and can be the primary interest of the book or the argument.

Skimming the index

The index will can help you to understand the book language. Well, studying an index will now not best provide you with an idea for the problem range that is being blanketed; but, it will additionally permit you to realise the opposite people the e-book buddies with, on the aspect of the used jargon. Perhaps, you can spot a few history knowledge that is critical for comprehending the argument.

Identification of pivotal factors

By this point, you need to have a few evaluation of the overall adventure that the author is taking you on and moreover of the jargon. It must be quite smooth a terrific manner to determine the pivotal factors of the related argument except identifying the corresponding chapters. As an alternate preference, you could opt for analyzing the first actual monetary disaster and look for a precis along side the locations of the principle elements. It can be appeared as a custom for the nonfiction writers to define the books proper inside the introductory pages.

Exercise

Try to take out ten minutes from your daily time table so you can carry out a brief inspection approach of the exercising e-book. Also, try and write down the vital factor takeaways.

Read

After you are executed collectively with your inspection, you could now get commenced out together with your reading adventure. You will must preserve the principle mind in thoughts. As you begin to check, you will have to supply the argument precis with you. In case the author makes a promise to describe the manner wherein idea performs out in diverse environments, that is what you need to assume to look as a reader. Effective readers constantly have a tendency to preserve the author accountable for the initial promise of the e-book. If, thru danger, you wander away after you have got finished with a financial disaster, now not having any idea what to make of it, you could use your GPS in hand. In easy terms, you could take a look at the desk of contents to discover how the author suits the small components into the arguments. In case you word that you disagree with what is being said with the resource of the author in your mind loudly, it's far suggested to maintain reading.

Keep in thoughts that reading is an act of empathy, and as you take a look at, it will in all likelihood be useful a terrific manner to treat the writer as an terrific pal of yours who is trying to inform one tale. You have to in reality no longer interrupt a excellent buddy only because of the reality you can't receive as true with what they may be saying. As you development, ensure which you mark out all the ones locations inside the e-book in which you feel confused or contest the writer's argument. Also, ensure that you separate all such locations from those that you fee and would like to hold them for your memory. It is generally advocated to take a look at bodily books with sticky notes of diverse shades accessible. They can act as a bookmark besides being a reminiscence tool. You can also segregate the colors – shiny sunglasses for the memorable ones and darkish hues for the confusing quantities. You can also pick a studying pill that gives the identical form of bookmarking feature that you may shade code too.

Reflect

As you get completed with studying a book, you are not simply finished with it but. It is now time to revisit all the tabs and then reread a few areas of the text. Now which you have heard the argument of the author completely, proper from begin to stop, you might now be capable of higher understand some of the components which you were pressured with in mild of all of the new perspectives or expertise. At times, you'll probably even get induced to reread a huge chew of the already-test e book, and this is absolutely k. Lastly, with the resource of accumulating all your bravery, try to write one small paragraph so you can summarize the primary factors of the writer and the book. There are folks that want to preserve a fixed of all their thoughts in the shape of a catalog in structures, which encompass Evernote or Goodreads. You may want to make all your references to the particular pages and then try and define the takeaways. Reflection on the newness of the related book, collectively collectively with your opinion, is important to your development inside the shape of a reader, except a logician. So, attempt not to pass the step.

Chapter 5: How Text Creates Meaning?

There is one puzzle this is needed to be solved in advance than you may begin your adventure of becoming a tempo reader. You want to apprehend the manner in which text creates which means. The primary distinction amongst those who obtain velocity analyzing and those who fail to perform this is rooted on this very know-how. Students who have masses of enjoy in reading apprehend thoroughly how written text receives converted into comprehension. However, nonreaders are regularly visible suffering, which additionally makes them doubt their talents, lessen their speed, and reread. As analyzing comprehension is frequently regarded as the foundation for the reason we take a look at, there can be no marvel that frequent readers who possess true comprehension will take higher topics from this education in comparison to the nonreaders. The statistics that we can communicate in this section can be beneficial for each nonreaders and common readers.

We may even communicate some hacks that can be used for unpacking difficult and lengthy sentences and decipher complicated writing.

Written Language vs. Spoken Language

As we have already said in advance, it's miles all approximately the publicity to published fabric and the studying frequency that allows in priming the thoughts for development in the arena of tempo analyzing. Keep a have a look at that we are discussing approximately publicity to written phrases actually and not a few issue approximately spoken speech. Also, you need to apprehend that it has no longer anything to do about IQ or intelligence. Some of the most well-spoken and clever those who are nonreaders often fail to expand tempo reading capabilities. It is due to the fact they lack the wanted experience with print and reading that commonplace readers own. Most human beings regard this to be hard, and there is a actual reason why.

Mistakenly, such people take into account written textual content as despite the fact that the writer stated some factor proper right into a microphone, and their free go together with the go with the flow of speech was recorded in writing layout right away. But it's far simply wrong. Spoken speech and written text fluctuate from every specific drastically. Because of the anatomical barriers of the human thoughts, even the most smart humans do no longer attempt to particular themselves in textual content-like complicated sentences using adverbial terms and convey their mind in coherent paragraphs. The reason that verbal expression appears to be a lot less complex in evaluation to writing is that the human mind is susceptible on the manufacturing of spoken speech. Extemporaneous speeches are frequently filled with mistakes, utterances, and repeats. Due to such a downside of the human mind, we are capable of every now and then stumble upon complicated issues furnished in speech with the usage of complex sentences, superior sentence structures, and entire paragraphs.

But most of the texts are full of such grammatical systems. That is the motive why nonreaders, who usually depend on spoken verbal exchange to take a look at, face a tough time while adjusting to the regulations of textual content that is in written format. Printed fabric can't be matched or seemed to be equal to spoken language that is written down. A written textual content comes with vital differences and recommendations that not unusual readers can pick up very effects, of which nonreaders are required to be made privy to. There is nothing to worry approximately in case you keep in mind your self as a nonreader. We will talk the vital versions in this phase.

Written Text and Its Advantages

A discovered out textual content does now not best will be inclined to make comprehension extra hard; it moreover offers severa blessings to the reader on the aspect of the brain of the reader. Spoken speech is fleeting in nature and additionally dreams the listener to strictly abide with the useful resource of the speaker. On the opportunity hand, written textual content can deliver a few feel of control as you, because the reader, can decide on the processing pace. You can gradual down on sure terms and phrases or boost up at some point of others. Also, you've got have been given the hazard to reread the equal subjects again if you need to, whereas you cannot often request a speaker to copy what they have got already said within the course in their speech. Another top notch fine issue of written textual content is which you have have been given the liberty to pause and discover approximately the surprising terms, if any.

Generally, we do no longer have the privilege of interrupting a speaker to invite for a few definition of any form of term this is unknown to us. In reality, written textual content combats all types of auditory bias wherein the thoughts unhears unknown words with the reason to live on track with the precept message of the reader. Punctuation is each different element that is definitely unique with written text. Learning to decipher punctuations – dashes, colons, ellipses, commas, brackets, and lots of diverse – is a incredible tactic that consists of studying comprehension.

Stumbling Blocks for Nonreaders

Among the severa roadblocks that nonreaders want to stand, like inconsistent punctuation and spellings, extraordinarily extended sentences are appeared to be the primary hassle. For example,

Whether inscribed on a rock, carved in cuneiform, painted in hieroglyphics, or written with the beneficial aid of the alphabet, the instinct to put in writing down the whole thing from mundane industrial transactions to recurring each day occurrences to the maximum transcendent ideas—after which to have others have a have a look at them, in addition to to to have a look at what others have written

In this lengthy non-forestall text, nonreaders could probable locate it puzzling to decipher the real because of this. In truth, they'll reread the lines numerous instances to make the overall hassle easy. We do not speak in speech using such systems of grammar. Additionally, there are readers who are ignorant of the way in which they are capable of unpack the sentence's because of this and destroy the same apart. In order to get to understand the unpacking mechanism, you may should discover how which means is advanced in any form of sentence. Also, for that, you need to be a speed reader.

How Are Meanings Created?

The syntax of the English language isn't always that hard. In order to boom sentences complete of which means that, you'll require primary components – an actor/ challenge and an motion. The closer the two additives are located in a sentence, the less complicated it is going to be that allows you to perceive them. Try to decide the verb, and the trouble on this sentence – Prince Joseph made a promise to Prince Adam to return to his party. Here, Prince Joseph is the problem or actor of the sentence. The actor is performing some movement, this is promising. The promise is the verb in the sentence. It is important that that verb and the project are related with each special grammatically in a sentence to make revel in. But what is Prince Adam within the sentence? Well, it's far the item this is receiving the movement, and "to return again to his celebration" is a tough and fast of more phrases.

Start Reading

The only way of combatting boundaries associated with prolonged sentences is to decrease the sentence. While we've got never been loose from distractions, from dealing with the ringing telephones and piles of mails to managing household issues, the distractions have in no manner been so overwhelming, voluminous, chronic, and intense as they're now. Ringing mobile phones are one factor; but, social media messages, email notifications, numerous electronic devices, and various browser tabs open are pretty some exceptional. The extra we're associated, the greater we are up for the neck of information, and the extra we take part within the warfare of hobby. We have a tendency to get engaged within the blur of multitasking sports.

As we paintings, we are dealing with distractions that come from every feasible path. So, if you want to rush examine and recognize the text's actual meaning, you may want to loose your self from the distractions. As you have got a examine, attempt to find out the kind of sentences in the text, the period of the sentences, the presence of punctuations, and then relate to the overall because of this. It will help your mind examine the text and paint an extensive photo of the overall content material material cloth. Try to recognize the number one components of a sentence, like a verb, subject, item, or complement, and further clusters will help to unpack the this means that quicker. All of those will let you navigate the difficult substances easily.

Myths of Speed Reading

If you've got were given ever heard of a person speakme approximately the manner wherein they completed fifty books in three hundred and sixty five days, it'd sound no longer feasible. Or, a colleague of yours finishing a fifty-net page record in a unmarried hour on the same time as you want double the time to finish the equal hassle. As you compare yourself with them, you may probably try to decide out the strategies wherein they accomplish that. It may also be the case that their time desk is packed similar to yours. Well, how packed is the calendar of a person has no relation to how fast they may be capable of take a look at. For instance, CEO and investor of Berkshire and Hathaway, Warren Buffet, can have a look at about six hundred – 1000 pages each day. How can a person spend a lot time analyzing? People who can simply fly through any kind of textual content can acquire this with the assist of pace-studying strategies. You need to have heard severa subjects about the concept of pace studying. But maximum of them are myths. We will communicate some of the commonplace myths of tempo analyzing in this economic spoil.

Reading More Than 500 Words Every Minute Is Not Possible

The not unusual studying pace of an man or woman is about 2 hundred − 250 terms every minute. In reality, there are adults who can look at greater than 500 terms every minute. Also, the amount of analyzing that any high-diploma government does is over 575 terms consistent with minute. Professors spend a brilliant deal of time reading, in which they're able to examine approximately 675 terms each minute. Of route, there are individuals who train themselves for competitions of speed studying. For example, Anne Jones, the champion of the area tempo-studying opposition, can have a look at approximately 4700 words every minute except comprehending approximately sixty eight% of the general textual content. As you start, you could not be at the volume of Anne Jones. There is not anything to depression as you may without problems beautify your analyzing velocity with workout and time.

You Can Comprehend More While Reading Slowly

In evaluation to the well-known belief, reading at a slow pace will not assist you with comprehension. In reality, sluggish reading can harm the quantity of text that you can apprehend. Comprehension has little or no longer a few element to do with the fee at which someone reads. It has extra to do with whether you may decipher and moreover preserve the data which you take a look at. One of the number one abilities that each tempo reader learns is to preview the available text earlier than reading and growth a mind map.

You Can Enjoy More As You Read Slowly

It is a totally not unusual misconception that it's miles absolutely false and has no basis in any respect. As you observe slowly, your mind can get distracted extra without issues. It may additionally result in boredom, in which you turns into liberating your mind to wander spherical. Try to consider it on this manner – you will never download a few movie and try and watch it in slow movement. The same factor applies to reading. As you keep a quick tempo at the equal time as reading a piece record or novel, it could make the take a look at extra energizing. Speed reading is all approximately green reading. As you have got a study rapid, you will be a higher reader. Also, you could get extra delight alongside element which means out of the articles, books, and blogs which you study. In reality, there are folks that growth massive love for studying simplest as they discover ways to tempo observe.

You Will Have to Skip Words to Read Faster

As you tempo look at, you could should organization terms together instead of skipping them. It may probably seem that phrase grouping is not any better than word skipping; but, it is able to do the trick. How you can attain that is a few different super approach of pace studying which you have already determined out within the previous chapters.

Speed Reading Is Supernatural

Any character can look at the techniques wherein they may be capable of tempo have a look at. Try to assume what it'd experience like if you may get through any form of textbook as you look at the techniques of reading about 1500 terms or extra every minute, similar to any not unusual velocity reader. Speed analyzing also can beautify your comprehension, beautify your competencies of productiveness, and guide your memory. All of these are enough motives to attempt out the technique of speed studying.

Slow Reading Can Enhance Your Concentration

People of these days's era encounter the majority of information within the shape of visuals and texts very slowly as they regard it due to the fact the manner to study, understand, and apprehend.

However, on the equal time, whilst an man or woman is given a unique to finish, he/she reads the identical at a faster rate and may nonetheless apprehend the precept idea of the story. You want to recollect that there are various terms in paragraphs and sentences that aren't that crucial all the time. They are intended to be observe for the mind and now not for the terms. So, there is no relation among reading slowly and interest.

Everyone Read at Their Natural Speed

Some humans trust that reading is a skills that we all are born with. So, it's miles often said that sluggish studying or pace reading includes us virtually. However, to think about this scientifically, it's miles been established that analyzing generates from reading. The competencies of reading could probable range from one character to the opportunity. For example, at the identical time as human beings stress a car, they stress at excellent speeds. The cause in the lower back of that is that they have got positioned to power in another manner, and it is not a few aspect that entails them glaringly. So, it may be said that there can be no longer some component referred to as "herbal velocity studying."

You Always Need a Pacer to Speed Read

A pacer can be seemed as a seen manual, like a pen or finger, that helps mark in which you take a look at on a web page. There are people who have a stereotypical picture of a person pace studying as a crazy-looking individual who maintains dragging their finger or a pacer down the web net page for the act of analyzing. But you obtained't want a pacer for speed reading. Using a pacer can nice be beneficial within the direction of the early stages of pace reading. You abandon just like you get a proper keep of the technique.

Now which you are properly aware about the not unusual myths and misconceptions related to pace analyzing, try to offer it a bypass for yourself. All you need is staying strength and patience. You received't be a draw close of velocity analyzing internal some hours or days. But you may studies the techniques inner a few months.

Chapter 6: Beginner Speed Reading Strategies

If you have in no way tried out velocity studying, you may surely be surprised after locating out how effects you may enhance your speed of analyzing and moreover beautify your comprehension. Reading greater than a thousand phrases each minute and comprehending the same in evaluation to a sluggish reader may sound impossible. However, it is not. In reality, it's been discovered that analyzing quicker and maintaining extra information may be less difficult physical than studying slowly.

Retraining the Brain
Well, the fact is that none folks located out to have a look at faster as we grew up. The possibilities are excessive that from the immediate you have got been first taught methods to take a look at, you've got been taught the studying

techniques which can be inefficient. All people have been taught in faculty to observe slowly; but, gradual reading isn't always a few issue but a stop end result of behavior of terrible studying. As you regulate the manner in that you look at, you could see a few proper away upgrades in your reading comprehension and pace. But why are we able to take a look at slowly? It is due to three matters:

- Rereading
- Inefficient eye actions
- Lack of awareness

We will speak a number of the vital issue techniques with which we're capable of decorate our pace of analyzing.

Learning to Speed Read

As you studies proper studying techniques and flip your new behaviors right right into a addiction, pace reading will become handy. As you exercising the contemporary capabilities, preserve in mind which you are required to be inquisitive about comprehension as you workout. The number one aim of speed studying is to adjust your muscle reminiscence and beautify your conduct together with eye movements.

• First, studies the proper technique of tempo analyzing. It can be better for you if you can hobby on one approach at a time.
• Slowly workout the techniques so you get to apprehend a way to do the same successfully.
• Next, you may need to exercise the trendy approach of reading at a great-rapid pace – so fast that you can barely understand a few factor that you examine on the time of workout. It is because the brain can device hundreds greater data than actually hundred – three hundred each minute. The mind does now not have the revel in of comprehending something which you try to examine at 10x quicker than your real tempo. As you preserve analyzing at this

pace, your brain will begin catching up slowly. Not satisfactory will you be able to regulate your muscle reminiscence and the way in that you float your eyes on an internet page, however you could furthermore modify the thoughts wiring for comprehending the whole lot which you observe at a faster tempo.

• As you exercise a technique of pace reading, you could now not workout analyzing as a terrific deal as you exercise eye actions. As you observe better on the facet of inexperienced techniques of eye movements, you can be a faster and better reader.

Strategies For Retraining Eye Muscles
The eyes take a photo, similar to a picture, of everything that we examine. As the eyes forestall at some precise part of the web web page, it's far referred to as fixation. Most dad and mom are taught to take a look at every word, so we come to be taking many eye fixations at the time of reading. Such not unusual

eye movements on each phrase have a propensity to slow us down. It additionally develops a mechanical barrier for studying quicker. There are sure strategies in which you can without difficulty teach your eyes.

• Reducing eye fixations and growing studying tempo: As your eyes get fixated on a few unique phrase, you could see a lot extra than the single phrase on that web page with the assist of foveal, together with parafoveal vision. In area of attempting to find to take a look at quality one or terms at the time of fixation, you may need to attempt to read three to seven phrases consistent with fixation. It can without problem alternate your tempo of analyzing. Just hold education.

• Practice eye actions: Take a fictional or nonfictional e-book and try to have a have a look at with higher eye actions so that you can increase your pace. In region of studying, by using the usage of seeing the primary phrase on every line on the time of studying, try and start through concentrating your eyes on the second one word. In clean phrases, the primary eye fixation on each line will start with the second phrase in place of the very first word. Also, try to fixate on the second-last phrase. In this manner, you may save you your self from dropping any of the eye fixations as you create an photograph of the easy areas at the margins. You will have to provide your self with mins to practice this.

• Stop yourself to reread: It is a smooth exercising that could assist in the removal of the horrible conduct that make you reread any text. Take any e-book and a pencil. Read one segment of the e book on the same time as using the pencil as a pointer a splendid manner to manual the eyes. You will want to glide the pencil on the same tempo as you development. You can't contrary your eye moves. The goal isn't to reread or move back. The pencil will flow into ahead, and so will your eyes. In case you can not understand what you have a look at, there may be not anything to fear about. Keep in thoughts that that isn't always the number one detail as you exercising and exchange your behavior of reading.

Reading Faster and Understanding more Concentration is the number one element of powerful studying, and moreover it is hard for severa motives. In the number one area, you have got were given your thoughts to address. The little voice internal your thoughts gets distracted easily and may get off course as well. You might also even want to deal with stimulation. We all apprehend that the mind can manner extra information than we are capable of virtually have a observe. As you turn your self proper into a professional reader, analyzing will slowly turn out to be a dependancy. Just like the use of a automobile, it is able to be accomplished even though the thoughts wanders. Even at the same time as it is possible to have a study with an unconscious thoughts, you acquired't be capable of apprehend the entirety as you take a look at without any shape of aware strive. It desires attention and all of your interest. Well, as you begin to velocity study, you may be able to absorb more records, and additional enter will visit your brain. It can even appear at a quicker rate. It additionally shows more simulation.

Removal of Outdated Ideas
You should have heard from your teachers or dad and mom that it's far critical to examine each unmarried word. Well, in case you live with such an idea, you are maximum probably to stand some difficult time mastering the rate studying techniques. While it's miles critical no longer to lose the understanding of reading at a faster pace, now not every syllable printed on the web page ought to be focused on.

Bonus Tips

When you get started out out with the workout of pace-reading sporting activities, you want to ensure which you study numerous styles of materials. You want initially the clean ones, collectively with moderate fictional or nonfictional books which might be clean to comprehend and observe. For the number one week, hold with the easy stuff. After you're finished with the first week, you can decide initially extra difficult books on your practice. Saying all of it all over again, you are not imagined to understand the whole lot which you have a look at at the time of exercise. The handiest reason you need to get started out with pace-reading sports activities activities the usage of numerous kinds of materials is to construct a dependancy. You might not want your thoughts to hurry look at only on the equal time as analyzing novels. You may also need to want to be velocity-reading any time you need to.

Keep in mind that the extra styles of fabric you operate to exercise, the quicker the mind will research. Thus, you may be able to solidify your tempo-studying behavior quicker.

Is Speed Reading Meant for Everyone?

Speed analyzing is a lot greater than surely being capable of boom your analyzing pace. You need to comprehend the data in a higher manner and hold the same for a long term. It is all that may be considered as a entire bundle. A very not unusual query runs thru the minds of every body who are willing to get started out with speed reading – Is it supposed for anybody? For instance, you're concerned inside the IT location as a part of your profession. With the speedy change of technology, you will have to live updated with all kinds of present day tendencies and information. Also, you may need to examine a number of technical manuals. Speed studying will will permit you to live knowledgeable in any shape of competitive commercial enterprise company in which you may also have masses of time to spare. However, a captivating part of being a pace reader is all of the factor blessings that you can revel in.

Besides acquiring a current capacity to keep records and realise higher as you examine quicker, you could revel in diverse forms of extra advantages. The introduced advantages will truely answer your query. You will get the answer that, sure, tempo analyzing is a manner that can be acquired thru any man or woman. All you need is exercise and endurance. Let us have a look at the extra blessings that make it the selection supposed for each one humans.

Better Memory
Your mind may be regarded as a muscle. In case you educate your brain, it'll keep

developing more potent, and it'll gain the capability to carry out better. Speed analyzing can venture your thoughts to start acting at an lousy lot better tiers. As you teach the mind to without a doubt receive all styles of records quicker, exceptional additives of the thoughts may also additionally get advanced, like your memory. As you examine, memory acts within the shape of a stabilizer muscle that works as you pace take a look at.

Better Focus

The majority of humans can take a look at approximately two hundred phrases each minute. It is regarded because the average pace of reading. However, there are folks that can move up to 3 hundred terms every minute. But what's the cause for this hollow? Well, there are essential motives in the returned of this. The first one is that the traditional style of reading that we are taught isn't in any respect efficient. The 2nd reason is the lack of understanding. In case you cannot maintain your awareness on what you take a look at, your mind is maximum probably to wander. Also, your mind will get interested by numerous special thoughts. As you tempo look at, it could assist inside the development of recognition.

Increased Self Confidence
You can discover about any existence issue at a quicker velocity when you have the functionality to recognise and have a observe extra. As you decorate your capability to research and study faster, you may come to see that greater numbers of doorways open up within the the front of you. You can get greater options in lifestyles. The motive in the back of this is that each article or book, regardless of if it's far fictional or nonfictional, can assist in moving our consciousness. You can be able to see extra intensity to your lifestyles. Such

kind of newly positioned intensity can assist in boosting yourself-self assurance.

Better Logic
Reading is like an exercise for the thoughts. As you train the thoughts to look at at better speeds, a few splendid matters show up. Your mind begins getting extra inexperienced at sorting all kinds of records and moreover unearths correlations with considered one of a kind facts that have become taken care of formerly. The greater you could decorate your pace of reading, the faster the approach can be. You might be capable of see the improvements automatically on the component of common experience. It is because of the reality you will get used to quick responses to all the ones topics that would have taken a long term to approach earlier than.
Emotional Wellbeing
In fashionable, studying is a very amusing hobby. It can help in the reduction of

strain as it may get your mind off thoughts and problems that aren't beneficial or healthy. As you start studying faster, you will be extra absorbed within the to be had fabric. It will make you be aware of the data which you are analyzing. It is referred to as lively meditation. It is a kingdom of meditation that can be completed through performing some form of hobby. Such a country can assist in freeing tension besides improving emotional health.

Speed analyzing is a good deal more than definitely studying faster. You can also think about it in the form of an exercise. Just much like the muscle organizations get stronger with each day exercising, the mind additionally may be strengthened with every day exercising. All parents can choose the physical games. So, it could be said that tempo reading is some factor that may be practiced by way of using the use of truely all people.

There are groups of people for whom pace analyzing can act like magic. One such organization is university college college students. Students are the proper candidates for the method of tempo reading as they will be in the age of gaining knowledge of new mind and thoughts. Also, with the assist of velocity reading, they might take a look at various textbooks and that too in a very brief time. Another member of such organizations is system employees. The artwork stress that place of business-goers need to stand each day, particularly in today's competitive international, is giant. Speed analyzing can help them to go through severa reviews and files internal a short length.

Chapter 7: Online Programs For Speed Reading

Today, there are numerous sorts of online courses so one can will let you to growth your studying techniques. You will encounter numerous courses which can display you a manner to study at faster speeds. All humans can use the capabilities of studying so that we are able to have a look at a piece better, from taking all styles of text within the books to analyzing substances that may be used for our very own use. The structures of speed reading can advantage anybody inside the long time. You can choose numerous different methods of analyzing and know-how fast; however, the facts and publications determined online will will permit you to in the identical manner. A short take a look at is the number one exercise which you may stumble upon at the identical time as scanning the ins and outs of any on line speed reader which is probably generally free of price. Typically, a small passage may be observe at regular pace and then examined to discover your modern-day-day reading fee.

You will discover a brief comprehension take a look at that is done to offer accurate effects. As you started out out with any tempo-studying course, it is essential to understand that analyzing speedy and getting an first rate knowledge really bypass hand in hand. The primary aim of pace reading is to accumulate a higher balance amongst analyzing with right absorption of the related content.

There are severa strategies of improving your reading pace efficaciously. One of the approaches is to apply the strategies of a class. In this, steerage and commands are provided thru a supportive instructor who moreover lets in in tempo analyzing. A -day beauty has the capability of doubling and, at times, tripling the studying output of a gradual reader. The development is quite rapid, and it additionally encourages college students. However, the outcomes are shorter as they will be predisposed to get lost with time. Books meant for velocity analyzing deliver severa types of knowledge, and pace checks are meant to decorate the abilties in both regions. Speed studying books may additionally encompass CDs or DVDs.

One of the most latest and simplest techniques to learn how to increase your studying pace can be seen in online programs. The precise factor of the internet programs focuses on wearing sports together with using animated pics and texts. One of the blessings of the usage of a gadget to decorate studying tempo is that physical reading materials additionally use the same technique. The not unusual method makes it lots less difficult for people to interrupt the behavior of slow reading as they circulate to 3 on-line path.

Online Tools and Techniques
Online pace analyzing is taken into consideration a quick approach of analyzing. It comes with diverse sorts of blessings and also can boom your expert and personal lives substantially. It will offer you all of the vital equipment which you need for reading a e book rapid. Within a short duration, you may entire a massive novel that would have taken severa weeks to be finished. Also, you'll be able to have a look at professional statistics and different things which can be associated with the business enterprise worldwide very speedy. It can help in saving loads of it gradual. Besides this, it could moreover provide a lift to your statistics base. As you get to understand the methods wherein you may test without difficulty, you can keep in mind all of the facts that you purchased. Speed studying is a easy

system that online courses can help to be accomplished at domestic. The regular way is easy to place into effect and comprehensible as well. All you need is a everyday exercise. Giving a regular attempt is the critical thing as you get to understand the method of online tempo studying. Let us have a examine a number of the facts of the analyzing method.

Why does it artwork?

Here are a number of the stairs that will help you in analyzing the approach.

- Form: The form of literature that is written commonly follows. It comes with an outline, a proper shape, and a end. You will have a take a look at the advent and stop so that you can get a few concept of the overall content. It can help in decreasing the time that you spend analyzing the post. While going thru the strains, you can moreover test for the content fabric this is highlighted and ambitious.

• Chunking: Such a way of online speed reading will need you to chunk phrases on the time of analyzing. We all understand that it receives less complex to read as we membership terms together in region of just studying one phrase at a time. For instance, have you ever ever ever located the way in which you respond as you have a look at a collection of people? Generally, as you notice people fame together, you observe them as one organization in region of a single character.

• Hand motion: Do you recall the way in that you used to study texts inside the path of your formative years? You can use the equal method while deciding on on line pace studying. As you use your finger, it may help transfer your thoughts brief, letting you examine at a faster speed.

• Word skipping: Online speed analyzing can be effortlessly completed with effective phrases, like a, an, the, and loads of others. In case you need to decorate your tempo, it is in reality ok to bypass all such phrases. As you learn how to pass such small phrases, it will assist in developing your pace.

Tips for Online Speed Reading
There are university college college students and specialists who look for pointers so that it will have a observe quick as they're required to enhance their competencies of reading and knowledge. Well, there are 5 subjects which you ought to try to live a long way from.

- Early night time time time reading
- Purposeless studying
- Reading in wrong settings
- Reading the terms in thoughts
- Keeping in mind what you wrote in the intervening time

The majority of college students normally have a tendency to read at night time. Well, it's miles seemed as the hardest time to take a look at. There might be a good deal much less consciousness and extra confusion. Moreover, you can experience a gradual price of comprehension. You can nonetheless try to observe, and your thoughts will wander a few location else. It will simply have an effect for your pace of analyzing. Also, as you decide to look at in the incorrect settings, you are most in all likelihood to get out of consciousness or go to sleep. Regression is not advocated. When you prevent the above-referred to stuff, you can with out trouble note some brilliant variations for your velocity of studying.

Accuracy of Online Speed Reading Tests
As you begin analyzing the techniques of speed analyzing, you is probably curious to diploma your pace in assessment to specific people as a long way as pace of reading is worried. You can select unfastened on line speed checks with a view to offer you with scores. However, are all such on-line exams correct to

observe? Well, the probabilities are fifty-fifty. It will depend on who designed the test and furthermore the net website online on which it's far available. You can say that the net web web page is a reputed one if the take a look at appears to be a pro. So, if you need an account this is intention of your role as a tempo player, you may pick a readership instructor who holds the important qualifications.

How to test readability?

There are severa forms of loose on-line analyzing exams. Most of them will let you examine some passage and record the time you are taking to test the identical. But it is not enough to select a few on-line pace-studying exam. After you are finished with the timed test, you is probably requested some inquiries to decide how a tremendous deal you have absolutely positioned. Quick analyzing can perform a little right in case you fail to understand what you examine. An expert speedy reader desires to examine and don't forget what he/she has have a observe. It may be regarded because the real description of a quick reader.

The places in which you get online studying assessments may or won't be accurate. So, for you to be stable, and if you want to be a pace reader in truth, it is going to be higher in an effort to choose a expert teacher who will show you the strategies. All the ones teachers who hold a license ought to take an intensive exam. You can be furnished with real instructions in area of the general commands that you can find on a number of the web websites. No rely huge variety what the case is, earlier than you lookout for a trainer, it's miles crucial to pick out an internet reading test.

Choosing a Speed Reading Course
Speed studying is a exceptional ability for an man or woman to gain his/her profession. With the massive percentage

of facts that we want to assimilate every day, it has come to be vital to analyze the techniques of pace analyzing. It is extra vital truly so we're able to make the fine use of the to be had time. You need to apprehend that it isn't always great about analyzing at a quick pace. You might also even have to apprehend the content cloth fabric and be capable of maintain in thoughts the equal. But how will you choose the high-quality speed-analyzing course?

What are the techniques that you may examine?

The majority of the guides be privy to improving the reading tempo without paying any attention to whether or not or no longer or no longer a player learns to capture all the statistics rapid at a few stage within the route. You need to pick out a direction as a manner to provide you with mechanical techniques so that you can recognize quicker. Also, it want to pay attention on severa unique components, like assisting you enhance your vocabulary, so you can rapid and without issues capture any form of statistics.

Would you need to pick an offline or online path?

Well, every offline and on line publications are of the same level. But in case you need to investigate pace studying to your personal time, selecting a web route can be a higher alternative. However, if you want to opt for commands, you may be part of a few offline guides.

What is the price of the route?

The normal price of the direction will rely upon the length of the course and the medium as well. Generally, easy publications that embody primary strategies of velocity analyzing will fee round $200. The superior publications will price you as a lot as $1,000.

Keep in mind that it is not that easy to pick out the correct course of pace reading. Today, there is an overflow of net sites which is probably prepared to cater to you with software program application and short analyzing strategies. However, just a few of them really artwork. So, you can check for feedbacks on-line in advance than you make a decision to pick out out a course. Try to collect as an awful lot info as viable, just like the course content material material, the style dressmaker of the route, reviews from past university college students, the period, and masses of others. Competition may be visible in every area nowadays. Opting for an appropriate velocity-studying direction will allow you to to live earlier of others. You may be able to look at blogs, emails, books, posts, and magazines extra without troubles. It will will allow you to collect more records, and you may be greater informed.

The primary advantage of selecting a few on-line courses is that you'll be in a role to investigate without trouble with the least amount of effort. Such a talent assist you to in diverse life conditions. Also, the time which you store with pace analyzing can be applied for tremendous crucial topics. Online publications embody audio sports activities, techniques, and articles that can help you with out affecting your clarity.

Speed Reading Exercises
Here are some wearing sports activities which you need to choose better greedy of the method.

• You need to check your eyes. You can also enjoy that your eyes are easy; however, it's miles vital to be examined by an expert.
• Try to check the rate to discover how extended you can have a examine terms in line with minute or at any given time. As you try to pay attention to a while, it will not best let you accumulate your desires; but, it may additionally beautify your essential productiveness.

• If possible, try to stay some distance from movies. You want to state of affairs yourself if you really want to comprehend the method. Distractions, together with films or video video video games can effortlessly break your awareness on what you are trying to have a observe.

• The purpose charge needs to beautify up your pacing except letting you adjust your very very own pace. It all relies upon at the content material fabric.

• It can be better for you if you do now not even trouble to re-check what you have already got a observe. Re-analyzing can without troubles slow you down. It also shows that you'll now not be capable of realise all that you pay attention.

• As you study, time your self. Even when you have already mastered the approach of speed reading, you may should keep running toward so you can preserve the whole thing that you have already found and beautify your competencies.

Chapter 8: Speed Studying Sports Activities And Techniques

Use your arms

Or in that case, the tool in your hand, the pencil! It's only ordinary that the mind wanders whilst doing highbrow artwork (reading, of course), because the individual is extra of an 'lively' being. So on this 'exercising', you'll need to trick your mind by means of manner of convincing it which you're doing greater of a motor interest as opposed to the stupid studying, just so's the number one factor to try for beginners. Try following your eye moves with the useful resource of your pencil, hovering on the phrases or underlying them. That way, you'll stay focused and you received't need hours to complete your homework or your workplace artwork.

Move those eyes

Another issue that the mind has a bent to do, and that notably affects your reading pace, goes once more. What does that endorse? It technique that on the same time as you're analyzing, your eyes continuously fall lower back or three terms, making you lose valuable seconds!

In reality, eyes don't bypass linearly like we might accept as true with. Instead, they make little saltatory moves, commonly within the studying path but every now and then within the distinct manner.

And of route, the word excellent registers inside the path of the prevent after the jump. (Yes you may don't forget the attention like the ones spring leaping shoes, and you may excellent manner the phrase in some unspecified time in the future of the landing). So in desire to doing more than one little jumps, try longer jumps that can help you reduce that touchdown time. That way you received't observe every unmarried word of the paragraph. Your analyzing pace will decorate drastically in case you look at fewer words.

You also can ask yourself if that eye motion is their natural way to move, can it's miles changed or progressed? Well, you may ask your self why there can be continuously sorts of readers, sluggish and fast readers, with out doing any type of workout.

Some human beings spontaneously discover the importance of quick eye actions and therefore speed reading is form of the herbal detail for them, however really all and sundry can expand his pace reading competencies with the resource of the usage of doing the same component consciously!

Underline/spotlight crucial phrases

Every university pupil is aware of that highlighting critical terms will let you analyze a lot quicker. In truth, the plain black ink on white paper and the large chunks they call paragraphs are not only eyesores however furthermore and extra importantly an underestimated setback for the visible reminiscence.

In fact, there are 3 kinds of reminiscence: visible, auditory and kinesthetic. It is extremely apparent that kinesthetic reminiscence can not intervene masses in the method of analyzing. Auditory reminiscence is used while helping a conference or being attentive to a lecturer. However, to take a look at with the beneficial resource of yourself, you want your visual memory and food pace analyzing techniques.

This trick is exceptional applicable for university students, who will need to read the material multiple instances earlier than their tests. In the primary observe over, you need to highlight the headlines, key phrases and vital thoughts nice. In the second time you have a observe it, your eyes need to only attention on the highlighted phrases, and now not look at the entire paragraphs.

By using this approach, the time spent analyzing the identical material can be decreased with the aid of a trouble of to three. Talk about again! So if this tempo reading method is mastered, the scholar can be able to take a look at his notes or three times inside the equal time it used to take him to have a have a look at it as quickly as!

If you study the critical component phrases and you don't recognize a fine idea, you can pass decrease lower back and examine one or sentences to recollect the general notion within the back of it.

But there may be inconvenient to this technique. Many university university college students locate themselves highlighting 90% of the terms after some time. It all comes all of the way right all the way down to the lack of interest because of the dull interest that is reading. For this approach to be useful, you really need to focus on the essential issue phrases handiest and.

This trick is similar to the preceding one but it applies now not first-rate to college

college students however also to humans and truly every person who reads in stylish. You lose so much time over prepositions, spacers, and fillers while studying. No addition the least bit.

The solution is simple. Try to have a study the number one and the very last sentences of a paragraph, and the primary and last paragraphs of a text. In modern-day day, the most important thoughts are each referred to at the start or on the completing. The relaxation of the textual content is commonly a few elements or minor additions that acquired't change masses to the assimilated idea. This workout is top notch effective, and it is easy to use, so it represents a great first step for novices.

For instance, if you try this method on an extended paragraph but don't get the overall concept from the number one and closing sentences, you may attempt to examine a few extraordinary couple sentences within the middle, and you'll honestly get it.

Of route, the method is greater regularly than now not inexperienced at the identical time as coping with material of medium problem. You can't count on it to art work while analyzing complex college stuff, like scientific studies or law lectures. But I'm fantastic every worker can already image big stacks of administrative center paintings on the identical time as studying this phase, and recognize how heaps time he'll advantage, what number of hours he'll hold whilst the use of this velocity reading method. Paperwork generally includes an excessive amount of filler paragraphs and little useful records. The key to double your studying velocity is to learn how to hit upon important sentences and 'forget about' the relaxation.

Set a timer

Set dreams for your self. For example, you may say "I'll read one net page in 15 seconds" and set the timer. At first, you'll be too targeted on that timer and you obtained't keep near the whole thing that you take a look at. But you have to maintain reading.

The tremendous element to do is to exercise on fascinating books, easy material which you've study multiple instances and which you experience to have a look at. The truth which you have already study the fabric will assist you recognize the content material fabric, so you'll be tricking your thoughts another time into believing it's in fact analyzing double the identical old form of words steady with 2d, and it'll get used to the ones numbers.

To increase your reading pace, as in some other project, you'll want to exercise. Use the commands mentioned in this manual and teach your mind. You need to be affected individual, as this venture will want time and perseverance to reap your goal. Practice each day, and grade by grade you'll begin to feel the difference. For each hobby, you'll do more in a whole lot less time. Keep at it, and your advanced analyzing pace will will let you reap notable things!

Set a intention

The purpose have to be formidable, but viable. You can't anticipate your studying velocity to magically expand. It obtained't be clean to right now increase your studying velocity 3 or four times its everyday shape. You need to have a have a look at grade by grade.

Your studying tempo can and will improve from the first time you attempt our strategies. The converting is probably palpable. For instance, you could say "Usually I take a look at one internet page in keeping with minute. Of course, I'm speakme about a non-complicated book, a singular as an example.

Right now I'll attempt to use the strategies I found out and examine that same web web page in forty-five seconds." Maybe you gained't make it on the number one strive, but you'll find out which you're genuinely close to that reason, and with a purpose to inspire you. Imagine when you have set a greater tough cause.

If you aim to check one internet web page in fifteen seconds from the number one few tries, you'll discover yourself a long way from that target, and also you'll rapid get bored and claim that this complete speed analyzing trouble is a dull give up. Little by way of manner of little, you'll find which you're carrying out your desires and exceeding them. And of direction, your studying curve will examine via.

Test your analyzing

Of path, it's no longer great approximately pace analyzing! The thing within the lower back of this tempo reading concept is to take a look at speedy, on the manner to take a look at quicker and extra very well. For college college students, it's no longer enough to boom your reading pace.

A little test can be completed in that context. You can take comparable lectures and try brilliant techniques to have a examine them. The first technique is the same old analyzing, it's going to take you to three hours to complete analyzing and assimilating it.

For the second lecture, attempt making use of these pace reading strategies, you'll spend at most half of that time analyzing it. And you could spend the rest of the time rereading the cloth, and therefore assimilate an increasing number of of its content material fabric fabric, or look at awesome lectures and substances, that is further as useful.

The significance of eye sports activities

Let's get everything right away; all the strategies and strategies elaborated on this guide are important and complementary. But the motive we selected eye associated wearing events to complex is due to the truth eye movements are probably the maximum crucial pillar of the concept of velocity reading. If you control your eye actions nicely enough, you've got were given got a shot at turning into a speed reader. If your eye moves are defective, there's little risk you becomes a amazing tempo reader, even in case you workout all of the other techniques and master them.

But how may additionally want to I educate my eyes, You would possibly probable ask. Eye movements are controlled with the aid of six skeletal muscles nestled spherical the attention. So, to boom your eyes' agility and precision, you need to train the ones muscular tissues like you would your one of a kind muscle organizations. No, you received't deliver weights together with your inferior rectus muscle, obviously, however there are physical sports suitable for your eye muscle tissue which you need to get privy to.

Glance from index to index

Stretch your fingers on every facet of you, and stick up your indexes as if you are pointing to a few component on the street. The aim of this exercising is to widen your peripheral imaginative and prescient by strengthening your eye muscle tissues. You can either sit on a chair or arise, something is greater comfortable for you.

Stay in the position formerly defined, and try glancing at your prolonged hands from side to side by way of transferring your eyes on my own, with out transferring your head. Glance quickly from index to index, ten instances on a row. This is called a cycle.

Now in each education consultation, you want to do this cycle three times in a row, and also you need to do 3 to five education sessions in step with day, it doesn't take too extended. On the number one few times, you'll sense awkward and disoriented. Your eyes might also moreover additionally even damage a chunk. But speedy enough, you may experience that your eyes have become agiler, and with a view to in the long run have an effect in your reading velocity surely.

Write along with your eyes

Well, we are metaphorically speakme, of direction, even as talking about writing with the eyes. Normally, there are smooth guidelines that the eyes take whilst moving; left, right, up and down. When you watch television, test, or do every different hobby, your eyes skip slowly in a single route or from one course to a few different (like while you're searching sports for example) or are extra or much less constant in vicinity (like even as you're searching TV or speaking with distinct people).

This workout is straightforward, in reality. Stare on the wall handling you, and don't forget that you are writing your call on that wall together along with your eyes. You can 'write' brilliant phrases, in particular fonts and sizes. And you have to attempt growing your speed on every occasion you repeat the exercise.

The factor from this education is that it makes you flow your eyes in nontraditional methods. You will pass some 'lazy' muscle corporations. And at the same time as your eye muscle groups get robust enough to permit the attention to move freely and rapid from one route to the opposite, velocity analyzing will become a bit of cake. The transition a number of the surrender of a line to the start of each different will cross without trouble and fast enough, it received't have an impact to your reading pace.

Enhance your peripheral vision
This should probable appear to be a loose idea, however widening your peripheral imaginative and prescient is feasible and rather useful for folks that need to end up tempo readers. In fact, as we have got defined in preceding chapters, ordinary readers study the content cloth in a linear manner, phrase via word. Their eyes reputation on each word at a time, on occasion at every letter or syllabus at a time, and that's time consummating. The peripheral

vision is each records that your thoughts options up out of your eyesight range on the identical time as you're focused on a single object. This records is commonly discarded as vain, so how can a huge peripheral imaginative and prescient help in pace analyzing?

The fact is, at the equal time as studying, the eyes make little pauses at some point of which the seen data is processed, and that pause, that lasts around 0.2 to zero.Five seconds, is what takes up the most of the reading time. Regular readers reputation at the word itself at the same time as analyzing, the pause takes vicinity while they will be looking at that phrase. Speed readers alternatively recognition at the little location amongst phrases and their huge peripheral imaginative and prescient allow them to look the two terms separated thru that region. That manner, velocity readers lessen the widespread fashion of pauses their eyes make via half of, therefore the large enhance of their analyzing speed.

Relax your eyes

Every exercising software program program desires rest days. And your eye muscle mass need rest too after this heaps exercising. Simply final your eyes does lighten up them, but there are extra effective strategies which you need to do after trying our eye muscle strengthening strategies.

• Eye squeezing

This exercising takes a couple of minutes, and its effect is positive on the functionality of your eye muscle groups. You start with the aid of beginning your eyes, and mouth auxiliary in case you need to paintings in your first rate facial muscle corporations too, as extensive as viable. After this number one factor in that you stretch your muscle agencies absolutely well, you want to squeeze your eyes as tight as feasible, and similar to the first segment, you can settlement all of your face muscular tissues too.

• Hooded eyes

Strictly for relaxing competencies. Close your eyes midway, and deal with your eyelids. Try to prevent them from trembling, that is the spontaneous trouble for them in that function. Believe it or now not, this permits your eyes to loosen up immensely.

Mental techniques

Do not vocalize
The maximum common blunders that gradual readers do is they check the content material fabric using their 'thoughts voice' like they're analyzing aloud in a look at room or within the center of a convention. You pronounce the word, you concentrate it being spoken in your thoughts. The hassle is that studying aloud takes greater time as your thoughts tries to characteristic intonation well and to test fluently, which isn't always in any respect crucial while you're reading silently. You must only interest at the content material

material, no longer on that nonsense. Some people even flow your lips whilst reading on my own, as although they're genuinely studying aloud, however with out generating any voice.

You should not pronounce the phrase. You ought to probable say that vocalization is a spontaneous addiction that you do with out thinking about it, and you may't alternate it with out troubles. But I guarantee you, you can exchange it. Here are some strategies that you may attempt a good way to stop 'pronouncing' the phrase, and begin reading more short.

You have to mention it earlier than you begin reading. 'I received't talk whilst analyzing'. While reading you have got to test your self every few moments. In the begin, you'll locate which you slip often and fast, you received't even cope with the phrases you're studying. Your primary undertaking might be preventing that voice to your head. After few tries, you'll discover that you're getting higher at this at an awesome fee. In an hour or , you'll get the draw close of it, and your studying tempo will growth appreciably. In an hour, you'll read triple the quantity you used to observe.

The key to studying this approach is sheer will electricity. It's about believing that you may genuinely flip off that voice for your head. You can attempt to assist your self by means of chewing gum or perhaps buzzing quietly to your self. That way you obtained't say the phrases, you'll fine read them, or even beginners can speedy get the draw close of this approach and increase their analyzing speed in just a few hours of education.

Concentration is essential

Concentration is vital so that it will acquire first-rate things. Unfortunately, at the same time as studying, the human mind has a unethical to wander and to focus on different futile factors. Usually, you may be analyzing, and then you definately could recognize that you've been studying mechanically for the previous couple of mins, so you could want to reread some of that material your thoughts selected to skip. That's a large waste of time, and that might even discourage you and prompt you to prevent! To concentrate, you need to create a work outstanding surroundings. No Facebook, no Twitter, no talking to colleagues. And with real lighting and a peaceful environment, you will double your studying pace, and with that, you'll triple the mastering you benefit in the same time slot!

But it's not satisfactory approximately the artwork surroundings and outdoor conditions. YOU want to interest. You need to remind your self each brief whilst that you are studying, which you are pace studying, and which you want to observe the whole thing you could from that content fabric you check.

Internal distractions are further as unstable. If you're analyzing at the same time as reliving the argument you had together collectively together with your buddy or thinking about what to position on day after today to the membership, you received't progress a good deal. You need to smooth your mind of all subjects that fear you or trouble you and cognizance on one and brilliant assignment, this is studying speedy and mastering the whole lot you could.

All the strategies indexed in this manual are useful and important. But with out attention, there can simply be no pace reading in any respect.

Don't regress

Regression is also a commonplace errors that maximum humans do unconsciously. Going once more may endorse which you're not information what you're studying. In that case, you may cross again a hint to recognize the content material. But in most instances, you pass once more spontaneously even though you're know-how what you're studying as even though your mind is 'ensuring' that it's analyzing correctly, so it's miles going lower back few phrases or sentences to comprehend the that means.

In reality, we're able to even say that regression is a sign of laziness of the mind. Your mind is positive it is able to skip once more at any second to reread the cloth and may loosen up at instances. Because why no longer? Even in case your attention drops, you'll without a doubt skip lower back and study once more. Well, that could't be happening once more. This is a big waste of time as it additionally affects attention, and you need to fight it!

There are few tricks that you may strive, and for you to in reality help you put off that nasty dependancy. You can cover the terms which you study together together with your hand, and your hand will improvement at the same tempo of your studying. If your hand is truely too distracting or is blocking off an excessive amount of place, you may use a pen or a pointer. This technique will help you combat regression, and it will also will permit you to manage your reading speed, as your eyes will adapt to the rate with that you glide the pen, and therefore you'll be reading quicker.

Practice this technique. Try it with an easy book, as you constantly do with a state-of-the-art pace analyzing technique. Cover what you're studying and try to preserve targeted and to consciously prevent yourself from regressing. Yes, at the beginning, it will want a aware try from you, however little by little you'll locate your self studying with out going another time even as now not having to repeat it to your mind 'I received't move lower decrease again… I won't waft decrease again…' Only then will you feel the real contribution this intellectual method is including for your tempo analyzing arsenal. You can also even boom your getting to know through a problem of five in a depend of hours.

Reading should be a depend of urgency

We all love the photo of a tanned body in a bikini, eating martinis, maintaining a e book and enjoyable with the beneficial resource of the swimming pool. Of path, studying need to be a laugh. Sometimes. But sometimes, you have got got hundreds cloth to study and too little time to do it.

You want to persuade your thoughts that you HAVE to have a look at fast. Always. That way you'll get used to that. You'll constantly study at a fast pace. Reading won't be a chilled bear in mind anymore. Of route, while you get used to speeding studying, you'll be able to set the pace you want, and you'll be capable of experience reading at the same time as you need to lighten up, and you'll be able to observe short when you have crucial sports.

You need to create an environment of urgency. It is a war you're wearing out to growth your analyzing pace. Push your brain to its limits and beyond. You ought to get hold of as true with that you can take a look at faster, and you will. With all this stress your mind obtained't have time to wander, your attention stages won't decrease, and your analyzing pace and learning will upward thrust in half of an hour, you can revel in the exchange.

Superfood for speed analyzing

• Spinach

Popeye will permit you to recognize, Spinach is right for your fitness! But it's now not first-class about bodily strength like portrayed within the famous cool animated film, it could wonderful decorate your highbrow capacities, and as a result decorate your analyzing velocity thru manner of double! This inexperienced vegetable is filled with nutrients A and K (potassium), that are essential to the law of electrical conductivity in all of the cells within the frame, particularly the thoughts cells.

In addition, spinach is a famous antioxidant, so it lets in evacuate the pollutants and the unfastened radicals which can be produced thru the cells, which continues the body healthful and equipped to art work!

• Broccoli

Turns out your parents weren't simply torturing you after they forced you to eat your broccoli, it's miles certainly a genuinely wholesome food, and it has a showed contribution in tempo studying. Like Spinach, Broccoli is wealthy in Potassium and has the equal outcomes at the neurologic tool in terms of reminiscence and attention, which, of direction, assist lots while speaking approximately pace studying.

And broccoli CAN be tasty! You can put together some appetizing food the use of broccoli, like Grilled Broccoli and Lemons, Broccoli Gratin or Mashed Potatoes and Broccoli. The give up result is confident.

• Bananas

Do we actually should deliver arguments to make you eat bananas? Bananas flavor extremely good! However, there's extra to them. Bananas are wealthy in Potassium and in Vitamin B6, which has a tested impact on reminiscence and cognitive features. Make a banana milkshake or a blended fruit salad, it's heavenly delicious!

• Red wine

Of direction, we're not talking right right here approximately eating a whole bottle in your non-public or drinking each day. The key right proper here is moderation due to the reality pink wine has great tenor in resveratrol which stimulates thoughts mobile increase and regeneration. Speed analyzing desires attention, memory, and immoderate mind functioning. And pink wine assist you to collect all that.

• Sunflower seeds

In many countries, Sunflower seeds have an indeniable region in every night and are even considered as way of amusement. In fact, they're pretty addictive and appealing, and the salty fragrance is specifically welcomed. So to recognize that they devise huge nutritive features is a big bonus. Sunflower seeds are a rich deliver of eating regimen E, this is an vital antioxidant that rids the frame of the pollution, and this is useful for lengthy-time period memory and may prevent reminiscence shortages and in the end Alzheimer's sickness.

• Salmon

Like all fish kinds, Salmon is a wholesome food. Salmon is wealthy in omega three fatty acids and therefore is one of the most thoughts-nice meals inside the market. Salmon can improve your memory and your learning skills. And salmon is tasty. Some recipes are actually nicely actually worth trying, like Tomato Basil Salmon, Baked Salmon, Grilled Salmon or Salmon Cakes (Salmon, Cheddar and Parsley Heavenly!)

These recipes can and will assist you beautify your reading tempo thru enhancing your reminiscence retention, and for a maximal mind functioning.

Adding salmon in your food regimen (and to the whole circle of relatives's healthy dietweight-reduction plan) has incredible benefit.

• Blueberries

Sweet, juicy, and heavenly delicious, Blueberries is a tremendous addition to a wannabe velocity reader's diet regime. Blueberries provide splendid quantities of anthocyanins, which are flavonoids, a nutrient critical to the mind functioning, cognitive abilties especially reminiscence. These flavonoids are well-known antioxidants that rid the mind of the dangerous pollution produced with the useful resource of the frame. They also are wealthy in vitamins K and C, so the impact on cognizance is nicely validated.

Blueberries ought to be part of every day's breakfast. They can be blended with any fashionable breakfast meal. Recipes to attempt the blueberry pie, blueberry pancakes, blueberry desserts... A satisfaction to all own family individuals' flavor buds and mind cells!

- Avocado

Like blueberries, Avocado is one of the healthiest and maximum delicious cease result reachable. There's a famous belief announcing that Avocado has an excessive amount of fat in it, that's why we want to specify that the fats contained in this fruit is on the entire monosaturated fats, this is the good kind of fat. More importantly, Avocados are rich in nutrients C and E, fairly favored for reminiscence competencies and attention, as already stated in this e-book.

In addition, Avocados incorporate folates, which may be critical to blood regeneration and ensure a consistent and constant blood motion, specifically to the mind. You can strive making guacamole, Grilled Chicken Salad with Avocado and Mango, and Avocado and Shrimp Sushi... Healthy and appealing.

- Dark chocolate

Yummy... That is GREAT information! We locate it impossible to withstand while delicious meals is likewise beneficial. Cacao enhances Dopamine manufacturing, and Dopamine can save you reminiscence loss. In truth, Dopamine based actually medicinal drugs are used in treating Alzheimer's sickness. Like most meals on this listing, dark chocolate has antioxidant houses and protects the thoughts against pollutants and metabolic waste. If you need to understand pace reading and double your reading tempo, you want to start eating chocolate whilst analyzing or analyzing, and you'll observe the difference. Of path, you shouldn't consume an excessive amount of chocolate because of the reality it is able to cause tooth decay or excessive blood sugar (diabetes).

• Walnuts

Like Sunflower seeds, walnuts are hugely fed on in great global locations. The number one perk in Walnut consumption is its omega 3 fatty acid content, like Salmon. Walnuts enhance mind functioning and memory capacities. They are also wealthy in iron, phosphorus, calcium, magnesium… those minerals have a first rate effect on brain stimulation and its most appropriate functioning. Walnuts also are powerful antioxidants, and are taken into consideration as wonderful 'unfastened radical scavengers'.

• Green tea

Japanese, Middle Easterners and English humans can be pleased. Green tea is indeed a effective device in our speed analyzing quest. Green tea is with out troubles the most recognized antioxidant food reachable, fighting unfastened radicals that siege the thoughts and restriction its functioning. It can with out difficulty be mixed in any food regimen. Green tea is likewise wealthy in polyphenols, which immensely confer to the safety of cognitive competencies which include memory and the prevention toward early cognitive decline. In our case, inexperienced tea has been tested as a splendid asset in our tempo analyzing trials. You won't remorse it, drink inexperienced tea after every meal, it may simplest be useful.

• Cucumber

In a salad, with grilled hen, or raw, Cucumber is commonly scrumptious. But that's no longer all to it. Like almost every inexperienced vegetable, cucumber brings masses-desired nutrients to the body, which include fisetin, this is effective in improving reminiscence and facts retention. Moreover, cucumber is truely wealthy in water, so it continues the frame hydrated, and everybody recognize that dehydration is the thoughts's worst enemy.

Cucumber has furthermore anti inflammatory moves, so it protects the brain cells –neurons- from degeneration, so it helps to keep the mind operating at complete energy.

• Coconut oil

Yes, coconut oil is inside the major regarded for its pores and skin blessings, as it is an exquisite moisturizer, pores and skin cleaner, or maybe a herbal make-up remover. It can be used as a frame butter, body oil or lip balm. But that's now not all there can be to coconut oil. In reality, this thing can have an effect on your mind, too. It works as a natural anti-inflammatory substance, lowering contamination within the mind cells, which keeps a excessive functioning diploma inside the mind.

Coconut oil is likewise wealthy in medium chain triglycerides (a fat kind called MCT) which help produce electricity, a bargain wanted inside the mind common typical overall performance.

You can also need to make sweet and crispy coconut waffles, or chocolate coconut cake, scrumptious and clean to get used to, and at the manner to quick triple your pace studying effects.

• Egg Yolk

Egg yolk is referred to as a deliver of protein, a far-wanted nutrient in bodybuilding and health sports activities sports. But egg yolk furthermore incorporates omega 3, which enables maximize your common highbrow capability. Eggs make a contribution to the coolest thoughts functioning, and there may be a number of tasty recipes that you may do with them. The fundamental hassle with egg yolks is that they've constantly been linked to immoderate blood levels of cholesterol, however greater trendy studies show that those claims are incorrect, so you can consume egg yolk yet again if you've been cutting your self off.

Recipes that you may try: baked eggs and spinach, salmon egg bake (in the ones recipes you accomplice beneficial meals for tempo analyzing, a win-win scenario), and of path, the traditional scrambled eggs…

• Mussels

Mussels are the right thoughts food! They are complete of DHA, a type of Omega 3, and vitamin B12, powerful nutrients inside the mind safety. They ensure an most best mind functioning with the aid of ensuring mind cell regeneration and constructing. Vitamin B12 is essential inside the hematopoiesis technique, the production of purple blood cells.

But that's no longer all. Mussels are rich in Zinc, Iron, and Manganese... Therefore, you could see that it's far an attractive multivitamin package deal deal we're speaking about.

The greater bonus: Mussels are smooth to put together. The classic manner to prepare dinner them is steaming. Once open, in approximatively 5 minutes, they're organized to consume. But you may get innovative and put together extra present day food with mussels, they are tasty and remarkable effective in growing your studying tempo.

Chapter 9: Myths Approximately Speed Analyzing

When we've been taught to read, in First grade, teachers have given us more than one commands approximately a way to observe well and a manner to observe efficiently. Those tips have been in truth beneficial, for first graders, but as we grow antique and get the hold close of this reading workout, we want to recognize that some of those commands are not wished anymore.

In reality, nearly the whole thing they informed us at that age is exactly in opposition to speed studying, and that's why ninety% of the populace are spontaneous slow readers and want the attempt to increase their analyzing tempo.

So so you can obtain the analyzing pace which you need, you want now not tremendous to recognise the only-of-a-type strategies to try, but moreover to understand the errors that you've been doing, well known them, and keep away from them in any respect costs. We'll be citing in this bankruptcy the maximum commonplace reading myths that save you you from turning into the fee reader you motive to be.

It doesn't paintings

Well, that's the toughest delusion to crack, and the most vital one, in truth. Because, if you can't persuade a person that he can accumulate a few difficulty, he in no way will. The first element I say to the ones non-believers is to search around them. If they're university college students, test your studying pace together with your different colleagues.

You will clearly find that a few college students study quicker than you, a few examine slower. If the idea of speed studying doesn't exist, why isn't there a famous tempo for absolutely everyone? You may additionally say that it is a natural knowledge, people are either born rapid or gradual readers. But we are capable of circulate even in addition. Why does YOUR reading pace variety relying for your highbrow kingdom? Didn't you ever notice that your studying speed at the same time as you're snug is insignificant compared for your analyzing speed at the same time as you're in a demanding situation, in an examination for instance? We'll assist you to contemplate the solution.

Sometimes, the situation is even more touchy. I've talked to lots of oldsters which might be willing to offer pace studying a chance but are searching in advance to the alternate to just 'show up' to them. They rapid give up and declare that tempo reading doesn't exist and they've attempted it!

Well, I don't want to burst your bubble, however that's no longer how topics artwork in the real international. Speed analyzing is a abilties. You may additionally feel a exquisite alternate from the number one minutes of attempting, however the actual impact desires greater time to take place. It wishes conviction, motivation, and most importantly, exercise. Like we said, pace reading is a ability.

And each capacity desires training and refining to will assist you to progress to new ranges. You won't magically growth your reading pace with the resource of a element of or 3. This guide is written so as to help you, but it is able to't and won't do the work for you. You need to be a hundred% devoted to the project at hand, and only then will it artwork, brilliantly.

Read slowly which will test more

That's the most commonplace 'recommendation' that teachers have given to their students. In truth, I hold in thoughts that a trainer used to get irritated with me for completing the reading undertaking quicker than the rest of the elegance. That modified into in 2d grade. And I bear in mind that from that element I've attempted to observe extra slowly and to ponder each word I take a look at.

As I grew, I realized that I didn't want to study at that tempo if you need to test. And then I decided the concept of tempo studying, and I located that it have become viable to study speedy and to have a study at the same time. Actually, tempo analyzing permits you to growth your studying velocity by using manner of double.

Another argument they present: reading slowly will growth your focus degrees. FALSE. Concentration doesn't depend upon your tempo, whether or not or no longer it is sluggish or fast. Concentration is a country of the mind, and you can thoroughly have a look at fast and stay centered.

Read every letter and every word for that rely

Like Myth(1), this a terrible dependancy which have been instilled in our heads with the beneficial useful resource of our important college teachers. They've happy us that we had to study every letter of the phrase, and every phrase of the sentence. Once once more, that is proper recommendation while managing first graders who're mastering to check. For grown-ups, it isn't beneficial in any respect.

In fact, research have proven that the human thoughts can with out difficulty decode the that means of a paragraph despite the fact that the phrases are not nicely written. The cause at the back of this weird reality is that the human thoughts doesn't paintings the way we'd figure it would.

It first-rate reads few letters and determine the because of this behind them, and moves to the following word. So, reading every phrase carefully will no longer help you apprehend greater, it'll best reduce your studying pace. The reality is, our intention turned into in no way to have a look at letters or words. Our proper intention is to accumulate meanings from the ones letters and words and bypass alongside facet that newly obtained facts.

Speed analyzing is great for clever human beings

I'd say the opportunity announcement is greater accurate. Actually, one of the motives why clever people are, in reality, smart, is they study quicker than most in their peers. They examine faster, just so they get more entertainment from the reading interest because of the fact they get to the 'exciting additives' faster. Moreover, the reality that they examine rapid allows them to have a look at extra because within the time it took you to complete a financial disaster, they've already completed 3.

Of direction, I am now not announcing that velocity studying will make you a genius. But I can assure that everybody, with a touch exercising, can practice those velocity reading strategies and improve their studying behavior. And who's aware about, maybe in case you make a decision to it and start analyzing hundreds and your gaining knowledge of tempo follows, likely you'll discover that the ones 'smart' human beings aren't that hundreds higher than you. With attempt and perseveration, the entirety is viable.

Speed reading results don't last

Well, I can't say that that is a hundred% fake. Like we've mounted earlier than, pace analyzing is a capacity. And any capacity that isn't polished and entertained will honestly fade and die. Like mastering a track device, or a modern-day language. You need to exercise for hours every day. And in case you don't, you'll often forget about about about the entirety that you've observed.

Imagine that you actually take a look at those techniques, and you see the difference speed reading makes for your worldwide. But then, the demanding putting that made you check those techniques inside the first place is over, and you start to lighten up yet again, and your mind doesn't discover sufficient motivation to preserve that immoderate degree of awareness even as analyzing and taking walks.

For college college students, we're specially speaking about holidays and breaks, after the tests are over. For humans, the remaining date is passed, the procedure education is completed, they are able to fall lower again into their strain-unfastened sporting events.

You ought to constantly examine fast and check your pace studying ability. You shouldn't permit your self fall back into the lousy analyzing behavior because of the truth there may be more disturbing events inside the destiny, and then, you'll be trying to observe rapid and to analyze faster. It might be a lot less difficult to be able to discover which you though were for the cause that statistics and that cut-off dates don't scare you anymore.

Benefits of tempo reading

CONFIDENCE is electricity

Reading offers you information. Speed analyzing gives you a fantastic amount of know-how. Whether you are at a meeting, at a celebration or for your lecture room, you could in no manner discover your self puzzled. There is almost no topic which you understand no longer a few component approximately.

From political facts to economics or even celebrity gossips, a clean tempo take a look at through the newspaper will provide you with enough information to preserve you nicely knowledgeable and will let you have a strong opinion in most conversations. You'll be known as a cultivated man or woman and an brilliant talker. That need to enhance your self assurance and improve your social repute.

If you have got been formerly a as an opportunity shy man or woman, you won't magically grow to be ahead and outgoing while you begin tempo studying. But the extra belongings you have a look at, the greater confident you becomes. You will begin to provide your opinion, and you'll enjoy that human beings admire you greater and are inquisitive about what you have were given to say.

That will work as a virtuous circle. You will revel in the trade of your photograph in human beings's eyes, and which will provide you with more self guarantee and lure you to do more velocity analyzing in order to build up sufficient statistics about each famous concern depend. You gained't experience awkward silences in buddy gatherings anymore. You may additionally have sufficient facts to both begin new topics or examine a person else's lead. In brief, pace reading will provide you with the guarantee you want to enhance your photograph and could be a huge improve in your self notion

An elephant in no manner forgets, and neither will you: tremendous MEMORY

Memory, like every cognitive features, has components: innate and purchased. The innate detail is, of path, natural, and varies drastically from someone to every different, and might't be changed. That's why it doesn't maintain a high-quality importance for us. What's extra large, is the acquired factor. This element is, thru using definition, something acquired with the useful resource of attempt. That way that we will have an effect on it through our movements, and improve it hugely.

Speed reading is in favored based on reminiscence. In truth, you may't be an terrific pace reader if your reminiscence isn't properly advanced. But happily, due to that obtained thing we were speaking about, the extra you train it, the more your memory will enhance.

Your mind works on a excessive degree whilst pace reading. In truth, we are capable of even assimilate the human mind to a muscle, and the greater it in reality works the extra it will become more potent.

You will enjoy the improvement. You acquired't need to put up it to consider your chores, or your homework, or the responsibilities you need to do at paintings. Moreover, you'll sense which you are becoming more quick-witted, with extraordinary reminiscence capacities or maybe higher data and faster belief. And the greater you train your pace reading know-how, the more your reminiscence will make bigger and it'll take you an awful lot a good deal less time to investigate.

Your each day sports activities will gain from this more suitable memory, however not greater than you expert existence or college, this pace analyzing advantage will take you to whole new tiers that you didn't realise might also want to achieve.

Rule #90 5, teen, CONCENTRATE! (A Hercules reference, for folks that didn't get it)

Like reminiscence, hobby is one of the pillars of tempo analyzing. To turn out to be a real velocity reader, you need to be focused all the time. And in flip, velocity reading is a splendid workout on your interest and step by step you get used to staying focused all the time and at some point of every challenge you do on your existence.

Usually, with this contemporary fashion of existence, we try to expose ourselves into multi-tasking robots, seeking to do all the duties on the identical time, because of the fact if we don't act this manner, we acquired't discover time to complete all the stuff we need to do. The problem with this approach is that your recognition is probably divided and also you'll best direct small fragments of your focus to every undertaking, and don't forget me, you may accomplish all of them, but they will truely be poorly completed because of the fact you didn't decide to every chore the eye that it merits.

Another hassle that people face on a regular basis is boredom. We normally don't commit all our consciousness to any interest due to the truth we lose interest rapid, and that is a form of laziness that is innate in every body inside the event that they don't try and combat it.

Speed analyzing can help you on the facet of your attention issues! In truth, as you exercise pace reading an increasing number of, you'll get used to reading at the identical time as being one hundred% targeted at the challenge. Your thoughts will then be aware of devoting all of its energy and hobby to the task to hand, now not simplest whilst reading but at the same time as venture every hobby. And while you are targeted sufficient, you may cease the mission in half of the time it used to take, and that may be a massive gain!

Boost your Professional CAREER

You modified into as quickly as a mean employee. You used to complete your monthly reviews in a single week. You used to put together your indicates in weeks. And your boss grow to be first rate with that. But now, you are a tempo reader. You have a look at twice as rapid. Your learning functionality has advanced. Your intellectual capacities have advanced; memory, recognition, everything. Your monthly reviews will take you three to 4 days in preference to each week.

Your suggests may be prepared in just a week, not two. Imagine your boss's pleasure! You turns into his favored employee; you may get all the touchy jobs, all the essential responsibilities because your corporation will trust you have have been given the needed capacity to do what should be finished and to fulfill your cut-off dates. In phrases: you can stand out.

In addition, as you examine faster, you will have a look at extra, and you then without a doubt definately'll have greater expertise. You will surpass your coworkers. You could be the quality candidate for any advertising and marketing. Even if you need to discover each different process, you will be prepared for any interview. You will blow the interviewers away together with your life-style, your information, and your self assurance.

The identical can be said approximately university college students. When you come to be a tempo reader, studying becomes so much less hard for you. You also can decorate your results, you could get a superb degree, and you'll be regular to an superb college. Speed studying will give you specific opportunities to excel on your destiny.

Real lifestyles blessings

School

The blessings right here are obvious. Picture yourself in that crushing phase of checks and finals. Every minute has its significance and may be important for your future. You have too many chapters to look at, an excessive amount of paintings to do, and you're not first-class you're going to make it. Speed studying is the answer.

Without pace reading: you spend hours analyzing a financial disaster. You don't locate time to do annals or to check the assets you positioned out. You might not discover sufficient time to test all the chapters that you want to have a look at in advance than the exam.

More importantly, in case you don't study rapid sufficient, you obtained't locate time to rest or do other sports activities to easy your mind and replenish your strength. You'll get worn-out short, your head will harm, your eyes will be blurry.